MW01273457

EMPOWERED
TO
LIVE

REALIGNING YOUR LIFE WITH GOD'S
TRUTHS WILL CAUSE YOU TO LIVE WITH
AUTHORITY, FREEDOM AND PURPOSE!

WITH LIFE COACH AND PASTOR,
Lucie Costa

WESTBOW
PRESS®
A DIVISION OF THOMAS NELSON
& ZONDERVAN

WestBow Press books may be ordered through booksellers or by contacting:

WestBow Press
A Division of Thomas Nelson & Zondervan
1663 Liberty Drive
Bloomington, IN 47403
www.westbowpress.com
844-714-3454

ISBN: 978-1-6642-3642-4 (sc)
ISBN: 978-1-6642-3643-1 (hc)
ISBN: 978-1-6642-3641-7 (e)

Library of Congress Control Number: 2021911342

Print information available on the last page.

WestBow Press rev. date: 7/2/2021

I dedicate this book to the love of my life, my husband, Aldo. He was my biggest cheerleader in everything I did. He believed in me, in my ministry and life coaching work through which I have the honor, privilege, and pleasure of helping so many people find and fulfill their God-given purpose on this earth.

Every day, he asked me how my book was coming along. I'm grateful for the way he gently pushed me to take great steps of faith to accomplish this and so many things I was afraid to venture forward in.

The manuscript was edited and finalized in September 2020 (thanks to my wonderful friend and editor, Rachel Hall: I couldn't have done this without you). My beloved Aldo passed away one month later. As a result of his wisdom and encouragement to me, I am getting this book out to you.

I'm equally thankful for my kids Nicole and my son in law Micah and my son, Micah, who have always supported me and encouraged me to keep life coaching and to write this book even on days when I felt overwhelmed. Aldo and my kids heard me share with them time and time again all that's written here. And every time, they'd say, "Write the book!"

So here it is.

I pray you will glean nuggets of truth from it that help bring you closer to fulfilling the great plans God has for your life. May you walk in and enjoy the freedom that God offers you!

Lucie Costa

CONTENTS

Living life on purpose is the greatest and most fulfilling way to live. Being empowered by God's truths enables you to live life with meaning at the very core of who you are.

You are loved unconditionally by God. You are stronger than you think. You are more than meets the eye. You have been designed to live on purpose for a purpose. It's your time to get empowered and really live the life God has created you to live!

AUTHOR'S PREFACE

I want to share truths from God's word based on a collection of conversations that have found their way into many of my life coaching sessions that I believe that could just change your life!

Digging into these topics and not being afraid of what will be uncovered often leaves my clients and me in awe of the deep works of grace God does as He leads us through each session.

We have wrestled through some of these, explored the possibilities of others and in some moments, just simply acknowledged the truth or the lie that lay behind them. Inviting Holy Spirit into these times of discovery and reflection has allowed many to become honest, authentic individuals who today walk in the freedom and destiny God has called them to.

As you read through areas that touch the physical, spiritual, and emotional realms of your life, my prayer is that truths you need to know will resonate within you and will cause you to become empowered to live! I pray that you will become free of whatever may be holding you back from moving forward into all God has for you!

I pray you'll pause and allow Holy Spirit to shine His light on the areas of your life He wants to breathe His life into. Genesis 2:7 says: "Then the LORD God formed a man from the dust of the ground and breathed into his nostrils the breath of life, and the man became a living being" (NIV). When God breathed His breath of life into Adam's nostril, He intended for man to not just exist, but to live! God's intent is still the same for you and me today. Are you ready to live?

It's my heart's desire that you be empowered to live your life on purpose and live it well with Jesus.

~Lucie Costa

FIRST THINGS FIRST…

THE GOAL: TO EXPLORE GOD'S THOUGHTS TOWARD YOU

Do you know God's thoughts *abound* toward you? What does that even mean?

That means He thinks a lot about you and it's all good!

In a time where people seem to be primarily into and about themselves, you need to know how much God is really into you! Everything God has done for you is to demonstrate His unconditional, never ending love toward you. And His *good* thoughts about you started right at the very beginning of you… Let's take a look.

> How precious are your thoughts about me, O God.
> > They cannot be numbered!
> > I can't even count them;
> > they outnumber the grains of sand!
> > And when I wake up,
> > you are still with me! (Psalm 139:17–18 NLT)

I love how the Passion Translation describes the same scripture:

> Every single moment you are thinking of me!
> > How precious and wonderful to consider
> > that you cherish me constantly in your every thought!
> > O God, your desires toward me are more
> > than the grains of sand on every shore!

When I awake each morning, you're still with me. (Psalm 139:17–18 TPT)

God's thoughts toward you are precious.

The definition of the word *precious* from *Merriam Webster Dictionary* is:

1. of great value or high price precious jewels
2. highly esteemed or cherished

From *Oxford Language Dictionary*:

1. (of an object, substance, or resource) of great value; not to be wasted or treated carelessly.
2. Greatly loved or treasured by someone.

This is what God thinks about YOU! He thinks you are of great value. You are not to be treated carelessly. Your life is not to be wasted. He cherishes you and holds you in high esteem. You are greatly loved and treasured. Yes! This is what GOD thinks and feels toward YOU! How awesome is that?! Every single day God thinks *precious* thoughts about you. Stay on that for a minute....

His thoughts of you outnumber the grains of sand!

Can you imagine how many grains of sand there are all across the Earth He created? There are thousands and thousands of beaches and deserts all across our world! Just imagine ALL the *gazillions* of grains of sand out there! Unfathomable right? His thoughts toward you outnumber all of them!

God's Word is *full* of thoughts about you. Let's look at just some of them...

He created you uniquely in your mother's womb and knew all about
   you before you were even born. He even says you're fearfully and
   wonderfully made (You are awesome!)

He created you on purpose for a purpose, to give you hope and a
   future. (No more wandering or wondering…)

God gave you His very best love, Jesus, so you could be forgiven
   and set free from your sins. (No more condemnation, guilt, or
   shame!)

God sent Jesus to die on the cross for you and raised Him back up
   from the dead to give you eternal life so you could live with Him
   for eternity. (What a hope! What a promise!)

He promises to make all things work together for your good as you
   trust Him and walk with Him. (God wastes nothing!)

He gives you peace and calms your storms. (You're not going to
   drown!)

He promises to never ever leave you. (No matter where you're at,
   you're never alone!)

He provided His written Word for you so that you could hear and
   know His voice personally and intimately. (He wants to be your
   closest friend)

God is for you and not against you. (He's your biggest cheerleader!)

He's already won the battles for you. (The cross says it all!)

He's coming back for you. (It's gonna be a great wedding day!)

If God cares for the birds of the air, how much more does He care
   for you. (He loves you more than a bird!)

God provides for you all that you need to make it in this life. (He
   is merciful!)

He calls you His friend. (The God of the Universe calls you friend!)

He gives strength when you're tired and joy when you're down.
   (Don't quit! He's got you!)

He picks you up when you've fallen down. (His hand is always
   extended to you)

And so much more…GOD LOVES YOU. Period. Unconditionally.

Are you getting this? Are you grasping the reality of His love for *you*?

You may have grown up in church and heard this many times: *God loves you*. You may have responded to His love and are living it out loud. That's awesome! Keep living for Him! He is faithful! Don't lose heart. Keep walking out your purpose with Him day by day!

Or you may have heard it, but to this day, you struggle to really believe it's for you. You may never have been loved like this before. You may not know how to handle it or understand it. The word *love* may not have a real meaning to you. You may have had a father or parents who didn't really know how to love you or who left you when you were young. That could have painted a picture of God that you couldn't trust. Or maybe you've been going to a church where it's very religious and you were taught that there are a lot of things you must *do* for God in order for Him to love you. You may know *about* Him but you really don't have a personal relationship *with* Him. That's where the difference is. Religion vs. relationship. Head knowledge vs. personal experience. A personal relationship with God is His heart for you! That's the place from where you get to see and experience His love for you.

Just picture God's love for you like a big warm blanket wrapped around you on a cold night. It makes you feel comforted, safe, and protected. That's the love of God for *you*. It's real. It's safe. It wraps itself around you and it never lets you go. How different would your life be, living from that kind of love? I bet a thousand times better—would you agree?

Knowing that God thinks that much of you and refers to you as precious is a great starting point for change, isn't it? **When you allow His love to be the foundation, the basis of who you are, life changes. For the good. For the best.**

Jeremiah 29:11(NIV) says that God has plans for you, not for evil, not to harm you, but for your good: to prosper you and to give you hope and a future. He doesn't just think precious thoughts about you, He also has some great plans for your life.

Knowing that you are that important to Him, what can life look like for you?

There are so many self-help books out there: life coaching and counseling books that try to direct you to "move forward" with your life and achieve great success in all you do. I'm not against them. In fact, I'm a professional life coach and I encourage and help people to read and implement advice from some of them!

BUT… the fact is, if you don't understand or receive within yourself *the truth* about the LOVE of God for you, then you're missing the most important building block for your life. If all you do is read self-help books and how other people did it, and you never believe and apply God's truth to your own life, you won't get very far. You'll experience what I call *stuck-ness* in your life where you only always seem to get to a certain point, and you can't go further from there. I want to help you grasp God's amazing grace and love for you so that you will be able to keep moving forward into *all* He has for you and live a purpose-filled life.

Many people I talk with have the idea that God is somewhere up in Heaven, and we are down here on Earth, and He just meets with us in church on Sundays and goes back up to Heaven during the week and is disconnected from our daily lives. But God wants to be at the very center of our everyday lives. **He doesn't want us to be religious; He wants to have an authentic, ongoing, *daily* loving relationship with us.**

He wants to give you a SOLID foundation for you to launch forward from. If you can grasp and apply His truths, you really can be all He's created you to be and do all He's put in your heart to do.

For in Him we live and move and have our being. (Acts 17:28 NIV)

Let's work through it...

Take a few moments and allow God to speak into your heart about what you've just read.

Consider the following questions. Write down your answers.

   ▷   *What do you think could happen to you if you allowed the words from Psalm 139:17–18 (reread above) to become absolute truth to you?*
   ▷   *What precious thoughts do you think God has about you?*
   ▷   *Why do you think you might struggle in believing that God has good thoughts towards you?*
   ▷   *What needs to happen in order for you to start believing how much He really does love you?*
   ▷   *How can you be secure in and sure of God's love for you?*

WHAT DOES ACTS 17:28 MEAN FOR YOU?

SECTION 1

Identity

Goals:

- ▶ Discover your original blueprints
- ▶ Embrace God's persistent love for you
- ▶ Drop the mask – You look just like Him
- ▶ Believe that you are much more than you think
- ▶ Don't allow anyone to hold you back
- ▶ Know the whole of you
- ▶ Choose to be His

BUST THE MYTHS: YOU ARE NOT YOUR MOTHER OR YOUR FATHER

1

THE GOAL: DISCOVER YOUR ORIGINAL BLUEPRINTS

———

Let's go waaaay back to when you were still hiding from the world—in your mother's womb. **You didn't understand or realize all the detailed work taking place, but something phenomenal was happening to you! You were being created by GOD!** You were being created on purpose by the all-loving, all-knowing, all-powerful, magnificent God who created the universe!

He loved *you* and wanted you to *be*. God loved you with an indescribable love even *before* you came kicking and screaming into this world!

This love God had for you from the very beginning is the foundation of your total existence. It's the very launching pad where you kicked off and flew into your whole future as a human being!

Psalm 139:13–18 helps us recognize this powerful truth. You can clearly see the loving, intimate handiwork of God in your life right from the very beginning, before you were even born.

In this passage of scripture, God introduces Himself to us as our loving Creator who put you together—*every single detail of you.*

> For you created my inmost being;
>> you knit me together in my mother's womb.

I praise you because I am fearfully and wonderfully made;
    your works are wonderful,
    I know that full well.
My frame was not hidden from you
    when I was made in the secret place,
    when I was woven together in the depths of the earth.
Your eyes saw my unformed body;
    all the days ordained for me were written in your book
    before one of them came to be.
How precious to me are your thoughts, God!
    How vast is the sum of them!
Were I to count them, they would outnumber the grains of sand—
    when I awake, I am still with you. (Psalm 139:13–18 NIV)

You were created by His own hands; you were "fearfully and wonderfully made." Everything about you is wonderful to Him. He created you just as you are supposed to be. Your eyes, your coloring, your big, small, or crooked nose, your long piano fingers or stubby short ones, how you would smile, how easily you would blush… what you would be good at, what you wouldn't be so great at…all of you was perfection in *His* eyes. I can almost see Him laughing with delight the day you were born, looking down and with a sense of swelling, Daddy-pride hear Him say, "That's my boy! That's my baby girl." You are His very own.

God created you with strengths and talents and abilities that would make up the unique YOU that you are today. He knew all of your days before one of them even came to be! He knew you before you were born!

Some Bible translations say He *knit* you or *wove* you together in your mother's womb. Do you know what weaving and knitting are? Let's look at some of the definitions.

    Webster's definition of weaving:
    • to interlace (threads, yarns, strips, fibrous material, etc.)
    • so as to form a fabric or material.

Some of *Webster's* definition of *knit*:

- to form by interlacing yarn or thread in a series of connected loops with needles;
- to link firmly;
- to cause to grow together;
- to tie together

WOW! Do you get this? GOD, the Creator of the whole universe, *knit / wove* you together with His own hands in your mother's womb!

***He firmly linked you all together*—your body, soul and spirit—so that you never need to come undone or unravel.**

He interlaced all of your thoughts, passions, giftings, and strengths to create the most perfect you. He created you *exactly* as you were supposed to be! There is nothing less or nothing more that could have made you any more perfect in the Creator's eyes. Not only is God the incredible, unfathomable Creator–God of the Universe, He wants to be *your* Father. And may I remind you again that He *chose* to create you. He is your Creator who knows exactly who you are and how to take care of you. It's comforting to know that no matter what happens in life, God *wanted* you, still does and knows you and loves you through it all: the bad, the ugly, the good, the amazing!

Let's work through it…

God took care of every single detail to make sure you were created exactly like He wanted and needed you to be. He loves everything about you.

> ▷ *What do you think about that?*
> ▷ *In what ways would knowing that God created you on purpose change your life?*
> ▷ *If you don't already know how it works, look up what knitting entails and imagine if you will, how God tenderly knit you together; every part of you on purpose. How does that make you feel?*

▷   *What are some things that you know He knit together in you that are positive and pretty great about you?*

REFLECT ON GOD'S HANDIWORK OF YOU AND PAUSE TO THANK HIM FOR BEING SUCH AN AWESOME CREATOR!

2

THE GOAL: EMBRACE GOD'S PERSISTENT LOVE FOR YOU

———

Ah…rich, beautiful dirt! That's who we are! Let me explain…

Picture this: God took some dirt - okay, the dust of the ground, (same thing to me!) and began to *form* Adam, the first human. Doesn't that sound a little familiar from what you just read from Psalm 139 about God knitting or weaving you in your mother's womb? Well, the first man God created didn't have a mom to be birthed from, so God had to use something to create Adam from. He chose dirt. Dirt. (I think that's a pretty cool and creative substance to use!). That dirt became precious to God and still is!

God used His same very own loving heart and His very own loving hands to create Adam as He created you and me. Why is this so amazing to me? As you continue to read this remarkable story of man's creation (Genesis 1–3), I want to point out a really important, life-changing fact that many never stop to think about, but one which I have found helps me to never doubt God's love for me.

In spite of betrayal

As God was forming and shaping Adam with His very own hands, with His very own heart, He *knew* that this incredible, beautiful human being He was creating was going to betray Him and reject Him. Stop for a second right here. Envision this picture. And read that sentence over again.

Not only was this human being going to betray His Creator, but all of his descendants, right down to us today, would have the choice of rejecting and betraying Him or choosing Him as our Father God. What?! Then why did God...? Right? I can't even fathom such *persistent*, pure love. And this is that persistent love that I'm talking about—that I want you to grasp for yourself.

God wants a personal relationship with us

If you had the power to create a human being *knowing* that he would betray and hurt you, would you? I don't think I would risk it, honestly. I don't think I could handle such deep pain. Nope. I wouldn't. But God continued to, all the while *knowing* this...

Why? Why did God do it? Why did God continue to choose to create the human race? I don't believe I have the absolute, correct theological answer to this question, but I personally believe it was because He already loved us and had each one of us in His heart. You see, **He wanted to create us. He didn't have to.** I believe He wanted *relationship* with us. God is love and I believe He wanted to pour Himself/love out into us, His creation. He wanted to pour it out on us, and He desired to be loved in return. I believe that's why we are so capable of loving. God poured Himself into us. And so, "We love because he first loved us" (1 John 4:19 NIV).

Free will to choose Him

You see, as God was creating Adam, He was also putting a *free will to choose* into him. Did you ever think of that? He could have put into Adam an automatic kind of robotic love response back to Him, but instead, He created man with a free will, a free heart to choose to love Him back. That's a kind of wild thought, huh? God would never demand man to love Him back, but rather He *desired* that man would *choose* to love Him back and to be in this love relationship with Him.

Now you know how the story of our beginning goes. (Read the book of Genesis to get all of it.)

It would be easy to think that it was *after* Adam and Eve sinned and chose to betray God that a plan for redemption had to come into place, but *God already had the plan in place even before Adam and Eve sinned.*

The plan was already in place

So not only did God choose to continue creating man, knowing that man was going to betray him, but *as* He was creating man, the covenant contract for redemption was already drawn up. It would just be a matter of time when it was signed with the precious blood of Jesus.

> For God so loved the world that he gave his one and only Son that whoever believes in him shall not perish but have eternal life. [...] For God did not send his Son into the world to condemn the world, but to save the world through him. (John 3:16–17 NIV)

God knew that only Jesus, His perfect, holy Son, could ever become the sacrifice to shed His blood for us to make us right with Him again. He knew what was needed and it was the ultimate price to be paid for us. He committed to us and came through. What love, I can't even fathom.

I pray that His deep love would begin to touch your heart and convince you of this great foundational truth: You were worth His redeeming, persistent love from the very beginning...

Let's work through it...

> God demonstrates His own love for us in this: While we were still sinners, Christ died for us. (Romans 5:8 NIV)

▷ *What does this verse mean to you?*
▷ *1 Corinthians 13 describes the love of God. Read this passage and highlight what God is showing you about His love for you.*

There is now no condemnation for those who are in Christ Jesus. (Romans 8:1 NIV)

▷ *How can you apply this scripture to your life?*

WHAT ARE YOUR THOUGHTS ABOUT GOD'S UNCONDITIONAL LOVE? WHAT DOES THAT EVEN MEAN FOR YOU PERSONALLY?

3

THE GOAL: DROP THE MASK—YOU LOOK JUST LIKE HIM

———

I'd like to dive into a question we often hear or ask ourselves: *Who am I?* I hope that as you read through, Holy Spirit will open up your eyes to see not only what a great masterpiece He created in you, but how valuable of a person you are.

Who am I? You are exactly who God says you are. You are more than you know. In fact, trying to describe you is next to impossible! Why is that? Because there's so much on the inside of you that you haven't even discovered yet for whatever reasons. You may have just settled into believing that you are what you see, you are what your parents told you, you are what your friends say about you. Nothing more than that. Or you just haven't bothered to give yourself the opportunity to really dig deep to find out what you're really all about!

Dr. Art Lindsley explains it this way:

> **Our worth is connected to our Creator. If God is of great and inestimable worth, then human beings made in his image must be of great value, too.**

Romans 8:29 reminds us that we are being "conformed to the image of his Son." Jesus is the perfect representative of the image of God, and we are being made like him.[1]

You may find yourself wearing many different masks throughout your life. Masks are worn to cover your true identity. Masks are worn because you may not feel comfortable with your true image, your true expression, your true reflection. Why is this? Why are you wearing the masks? Are you struggling? Hiding feelings of shame, guilt, condemnation, or brokenness? Does the mask really help? Maybe for a time, but when you do take it off—when you're alone—you still have to deal with what's staring back at you. Who told you to wear the masks? When will you become comfortable enough with who you truly are to take them off? What needs to happen for you to do that?

These are hard questions to answer, but in order for you to be healed and free, you must answer them honestly, with the help, love and truth that comes from Holy Spirit.

What are we believing?

We believe the lies that we're not pretty or handsome enough. We wear makeup and certain clothes to try to portray an image that is more acceptable to society. We'll fit in better if we look like "them." We believe the lies that we have to get more education, better jobs; we climb corporate ladders or get into an enormous amount of debt just to show that we can keep up with all those "successful" people who've made it out there! We cringe when one challenges: How dare one live and do what they are uniquely purposed to do? We cringe because—do we dare to? What stops us?

We get into relationships that we know are not healthy for us. We do things that we know go against our morals, yet we push through all of that just so we can create for ourselves an identity that satisfies "them" and they accept us. And so, the merry go round goes round and round

---

[1] Dr. Art Lindsley, "Made In the Image of God – The Basis for Our Significance," Institute For Faith, Work & Economics, March 22, 2016, https://tifwe.org/made-in-the-image-of-god-the-basis-for-our-significance/.

and round. When will you get off? It's spinning so fast you can't seem to catch your breath at times! **And what's worse is that while you're spinning, your mask is slipping and you have to try so hard to keep it in place.** It's spiritually, mentally, emotionally and physically draining. It's time to take off the mask before you spiral out of control. It's time to learn how to become comfortable and accepting of who you really are. And I want to help you with this...

God desires that you find your identity in His truth about who HE says you are. When you know the truth about yourself, your whole way of living changes. Your relationship with Him becomes more meaningful. You're able to see things from a higher perspective (His). You find your purpose and fulfill your destiny with confidence, knowing you've been created on purpose by Him and for Him.

To know who you truly are, at the core, is to know who GOD your Father is first. After all, since He created you, and in His image at that, don't you think it's important to discover who He is? To know who you are?

Years ago, the first time I read that I was made in the image of God, I was amazed. **Me? I'm made to look like Him? Wait! If I look like Him, I want to know: What does He look like?** And so, over the years, I entered on my journey of discovering what God looked like. What I found was a real, captivating, beautiful image that I get to reflect... and so do you!

Let's look at the definition of *image*.

From *Bible Dictionary*: (Vulgate: imago); it is derived from eiko, eoika, "to be like," "resemble," and means

1. that which resembles an object and represents it, as a copy represents the original.
2. the engraved stamp or mark on the instrument (passive sense);
3. the impress made by the instrument on wax or other object;
4. hence, generally, the exact image or expression of any person or thing as corresponding to the original, the distinguishing feature, or traits by which a person or thing is known.

God said, "Let Us make man in Our image" (Genesis 1:26 NASB). So, according to the dictionary definition of that word *image,* that means He engraved a stamp or a mark on us. He *impressed* on us HIS very own mark; image. **We are the exact image or expression of Him with distinguishing traits by which GOD is known.** What?! If this isn't blowing your mind, I don't know what could! This is an incredible revelation!

We *resemble* and *represent* Him. We are a copy (a reflection) of the Original! I am shouting and dancing on the inside! Are you?

So we discover that right from the very beginning, as God was creating Adam, that God was revealing who *He* is. He is LOVE. If God was not love itself, He wouldn't have created Adam because of all He knew was going to happen in the future. But He did anyway. That's LOVE! God is love, and therefore love created you. *You* are full of love. This is so powerful and empowering if you can truly grasp it for yourself.

What does God look like?

God is love. God is kind. God is compassionate. God is merciful. God is grace. God is peace. God is truth. God is forgiving. God is trustworthy. God is honest. God is patient. God is strong. God is loyal. God is beautiful. God is light. God is joy. God is good. And the list of who He is is unending!

The Holy Spirit is God's spirit who lives in you. **If He lives in you, *you* possess the very characteristics and traits of God Himself!**

I know this may be a bit overwhelming, but track with me: it gets better! I did more digging and found out more of what He looks like in Galatians 5:22 & 23 (NIV):

> But the fruit of the Spirit is love, joy, peace, forbearance, kindness, goodness, faithfulness, gentleness and self-control. Against such things there is no law.

There's no law that could stop Him from being who He is, and there is no law to stop me or you from being like Him either! Isn't He beautiful? Isn't He captivating? Who wouldn't want to possess all of those attractive traits and look like love and kindness and joy…?

That's what *you* look like! Just like Him… When you uncover and discover who GOD is, then you will discover and uncover who YOU are!

When Jesus came to Earth, He made this powerful statement in John 14:9. He said, "Anyone who has seen me has seen the Father" (NIV).

In the Word we see that Jesus Christ is the absolute perfect image of God the Father. When we "see" Jesus, we see our Father God, and so we can see ourselves—or at least what we're supposed to look like!

The tangible image of God Himself!

Let's take a few minutes then and look at Jesus, the reflection of Father God. He paints the picture of who each of us could look like. **It's actually possible to look like our original design.** Sign me up!

Did you know this about Jesus?

As you observe the life of Jesus, you'll notice that He is full of unconditional love. He is patient, kind and compassionate. He is also strong, confident, sure of Himself and unshakeable. No matter how hard people tried to hurt Him, betray Him and reject Him, He always remained loving. Although He operated from love, He did not tolerate evil and the sin that went against God and His righteousness. He called evil out and spoke truth when it was called for - with grace. He loved what God the Father loved and hated what He hated. He was humble, but He stood steadfast for holiness and purity. He was obedient to the Father's will even unto death. He loved and respected those He lived with and showed them the better way. He was true all the way through. He was full of grace and mercy. He took time to talk with people and to let them know about Heaven. He genuinely cared for people. He stopped and met people's needs. He healed people of their sicknesses and cast out demons so people could be free. He fed the hungry. He gave hope when there was mourning. He wept with His friends. He went to weddings and feasts. He didn't hide from people, but He made Himself available to them. He was full of courage. He was peace itself. He calmed storms and He calmed hearts. He spent time with the Father and had a disciplined prayer life. He taught, He demonstrated and was the very essence of hope and enduring love.

WOW! As I write this, I am once again amazed at who Jesus was and how He so graciously set before each of us the example of living a godly and purposed life!

The list of who He was and how He lived is pretty amazing and endless, but I think you get the idea.

Jesus is our prime example of who we were created to be and to look like in the image of our Father God. **What an incredible picture of the reflection of God we can be if we chose to accept this as our true identity!**

No matter what family you've come from or didn't, no matter if you've lived in poverty or in wealth, no matter if you've made the biggest mistakes in life, or you've lived the holiest life ever, if you find your identity in God, then you have found your true self! You really are made to look a whole lot like Him! **Why should this life-changing discovery matter? Because it is the foundation for your life.**

Let's work through it…

> ▷ *In light of what you just read in this chapter, are you ready to take off the masks?*
> ▷ *What do you imagine it would feel like to live your life mask-free?*
> ▷ *What does looking like Jesus mean to you?*
> ▷ *What areas do you need to change to reflect Him more?*

HOW COULD REFLECTING THE IMAGE OF GOD CHANGE YOUR LIFE?

4

THE GOAL: BELIEVE THAT YOU ARE MUCH MORE THAN YOU THINK

———

What do you think of yourself? What do you say about yourself? How do you see yourself? I want to take some time with you and go over a few things I believe you should know about yourself that *God* says about you. *Knowing* what they are and *believing* that they are qualities and absolute truths to live by will give you a whole new perspective of living!

Remember, God created you. His love was and still is pursuing you. He made you in His image and you're a pretty amazing reflection of Him!

You are so much more than you think!

His love for you is endless and who you are in Him is too great to describe in my own feeble words. **I cannot adequately tell you who you are, but God's Word can.** The Word of God does not lie. Everything it says about you is truth. The Word of God brings life. I pray that as you read what He says about you that you will experience hope, love, joy and purpose.

Get ready to discover that you are truly amazing!

You are loved unconditionally

> But God shows his love for us in that while we were still sinners, Christ died for us. (Romans 5:8 ESV)

For God so loved the world, that he gave his only Son, that whoever believes in him should not perish but have eternal life. For God did not send his Son into the world to condemn the world, but in order that the world might be saved through him. (John 3:16–17 ESV)

For I am persuaded that neither death nor life, nor angels nor principalities nor powers, nor things present nor things to come, nor height nor depth, nor any other created thing, shall be able to separate us from the love of God which is in Christ Jesus our Lord. (Romans 8:38–39 NKJV)

You are forgiven

If we confess our sins, he is faithful and just to forgive us our sins and to cleanse us from all unrighteousness. (1 John 1:9 NKJV)

He has not punished us as we deserve for all our sins, for his mercy toward those who fear and honor him is as great as the height of the heavens above the earth. He has removed our sins as far away from us as the east is from the west. He is like a father to us, tender and sympathetic to those who reverence him. For he knows we are but dust. (Psalm 103:10–14 TLB)

For I will forgive their wickedness and will remember their sins no more. (Hebrews 8:12 NIV)

But God, being rich in mercy, because of the great love with which he loved us, even when we were dead in our trespasses, made us alive together with Christ—by grace you have been saved... (Ephesians 2:4–5 ESV)

In him we have redemption through his blood, the forgiveness of our trespasses, according to the riches of his grace... (Ephesians 1:7 ESV)

You are called to be His very own

But to all who did receive Him, who believed in His name, He gave the right to become children of God... (John 1:12 ESV)

"I will be a Father to you, and you will be my sons and daughters," says the Lord Almighty. (2 Corinthians 6:18 NIV)

Just as He chose us in Him before the foundation of the world, that we should be holy and without blame before Him in love, having predestined us to adoption as sons by Jesus Christ to Himself, according to the good pleasure of His will... (Ephesians 1:4–5 NKJV)

You are a new creation

Therefore, if anyone is in Christ, he is a new creation. The old has passed away; behold, the new has come. (2 Corinthians 5:17 ESV)

I have been crucified with Christ. It is no longer I who live, but Christ who lives in me. And the life I now live in the flesh I live by faith in the Son of God, who loved me and gave himself for me. (Galatians 2:20 ESV)

See, I am doing a new thing! Now it springs up; do you not perceive it? I am making a way in the wilderness and streams in the wasteland. (Isaiah 43:19 NIV)

You are made free

There is therefore now no condemnation for those who are in Christ Jesus. (Romans 8:1 ESV)

So if the Son sets you free, you will be free indeed. (John 8:36 NIV)

We know that our old self was crucified with him in order that the body of sin might be brought to nothing, so that we would no longer be enslaved to sin. (Romans 6:6 ESV)

Now the Lord is the Spirit, and where the Spirit of the Lord is, there is freedom. (2 Corinthians 3:17 NIV)

It is for freedom that Christ has set us free. Stand firm, then, and do not let yourselves be burdened again by a yoke of slavery. (Galatians 5:1 NIV)

You are God's reflection

Then God said, "Let us make man in our image, after our likeness. And let them have dominion over the fish of the sea and over the birds of the heavens and over the livestock and over all the earth and over every creeping thing that creeps on the earth." So God created man in his own image, in the image of God he created him; male and female he created them. (Genesis 1:26–27 ESV)

And to put on the new self, created after the likeness of God in true righteousness and holiness. (Ephesians 4:24 ESV)

But the Holy Spirit produces this kind of fruit in our lives: love, joy, peace, patience, kindness, goodness, faithfulness, gentleness, and self-control. There is no law against these things! (Galatians 5:22–23 NLT)

You are cared for by God

Are not two sparrows sold for a copper coin? And not one of them falls to the ground apart from your Father's will. But the very hairs of your head are all numbered. Do not fear therefore; you are of more value than many sparrows. (Matthew 10:29–31 NKJV)

And God is able to bless you abundantly, so that in all things at all times, having all that you need, you will abound in every good work. (2 Corinthians 9:8 NIV)

His divine power has given to us all things that pertain to life and godliness, through the knowledge of Him who called us by glory and virtue, by which have been given to us exceedingly great and precious promises, that through these you may be partakers of the divine nature... (2 Peter 1:3–4 NKJV)

You are purposed

> For I know the plans I have for you, says the LORD, They are plans for good and not for evil, to give you a future and a hope. (Jeremiah 29:11 TLB)

> For we are His workmanship, created in Christ Jesus for good works, which God prepared beforehand that we should walk in them. (Ephesians 2:10 NKJV)

You are a light

> You are the light of the world. A city set on a hill cannot be hidden; nor does anyone light a lamp and put it under a basket, but on the lampstand, and it gives light to all who are in the house. (Matthew 5:14–16 ESV)

> The light shines in the darkness, and the darkness has not overcome it. (John 1:5 NIV)

You are fearless

> For God did not give us a spirit of fear but of power and love and a sound mind. (2 Timothy 1:7 NIV)

> Fear not, for I am with you; be not dismayed, for I am your God; I will strengthen you, I will help you, I will uphold you with my righteous right hand. (Isaiah 41:10 ESV)

You are established in Him

> But the Lord is faithful. He will establish you and guard you against the evil one. (2 Thessalonians 3:3 ESV)

> I waited patiently for the LORD to help me, and he turned to me and heard my cry. He lifted me out of the pit of despair, out of the mud and the mire. He set my feet on solid ground and steadied me as I walked along. (Psalm 40:1–2 NLT)

In him you also, when you heard the word of truth, the gospel of your salvation, and believed in him, were sealed with the promised Holy Spirit… (Ephesians 1:13 ESV)

He is like a man building a house, who dug deep and laid the foundation on the rock. And when a flood arose, the stream broke against that house and could not shake it, because it had been well built. (Luke 6:48 ESV)

You are never alone

And the LORD, He is the One who goes before you. He will be with you, He will not leave you nor forsake you; do not fear nor be dismayed. (Deuteronomy 31:8 NKJV)

Do you not know that you are God's temple and that God's Spirit dwells in you? (1 Corinthians 3:16 ESV)

For I am sure that neither death nor life, nor angels nor rulers, nor things present nor things to come, nor powers, nor height nor depth, nor anything else in all creation, will be able to separate us from the love of God in Christ Jesus our Lord. (Romans 8:38–39 ESV)

You are stronger than you think

Be strong and courageous. Do not be afraid. Do not be discouraged, for the LORD your God will be with you wherever you go. (Joshua 1:9 NIV)

I can do all things through him who strengthens me. (Philippians 4:13 ESV)

In all these things we are more than conquerors through him who loved us. (Romans 8:37 ESV)

But those who hope in the LORD will renew their strength. They will soar on wings like eagles; they will run and not grow weary, they will walk and not be faint. (Isaiah 40:31 NIV)

You are called

"For I know the plans I have for you," declares the LORD, "plans to prosper you and not to harm you, plans to give you hope and a future." (Jeremiah 29:11 NIV)

Then [Jesus] said to them all: "Whoever wants to be my disciple must deny themselves and take up their cross daily and follow me." (Luke 9:23 NIV)

The Spirit of the Sovereign LORD is upon me, for the LORD has anointed me to bring good news to the poor. He has sent me to comfort the brokenhearted and to proclaim that captives will be released and prisoners will be freed. He has sent me to tell those who mourn that the time of the LORD's favor has come, and with it, the day of God's anger against their enemies. To all who mourn in Israel, he will give a crown of beauty for ashes, a joyous blessing instead of mourning, festive praise instead of despair. In their righteousness, they will be like great oaks that the LORD has planted for his own glory. (Isaiah 61:1–3 NLT)

You are full of love

Therefore, as God's chosen people, holy and dearly loved, clothe yourselves with compassion, kindness, humility, gentleness and patience. (Colossians 3:12 NIV)

My command is this: Love each other as I have loved you. Greater love has no one than this: to lay down one's life for one's friends. (John 15:12–13 NIV)

Do to others as you would have them do to you. (Luke 6:31 NIV)

Be completely humble and gentle; be patient, bearing with one another in love. (Ephesians 4:2 NIV)

You are wise

> Therefore whoever hears these sayings of Mine, and does them, I will liken him to a wise man who built his house on the rock: and the rain descended, the floods came, and the winds blew and beat on that house; and it did not fall, for it was founded on the rock. (Matthew 7:24–25 NKJV)

> If any of you lacks wisdom, let him ask God, who gives generously to all without reproach, and it will be given him. (James 1:5 ESV)

You are an ambassador of Heaven

> But you will receive power when the Holy Spirit has come upon you, and you will be my witnesses in Jerusalem and in all Judea and Samaria, and to the end of the earth. (Acts 1:8 ESV)

> …God was in Christ reconciling the world to Himself, not counting their trespasses against them, and He has committed to us the word of reconciliation.

> Therefore, we are ambassadors for Christ, as though God were making an appeal through us; we beg you on behalf of Christ, be reconciled to God. (2 Corinthians 5:19–20 NIV)

WOW! Do you realize how incredibly amazing and wonderful you are? I can't repeat that to you often enough! Do you see how loved you are? How purposed you are? How safe in God's love you are? How strong you are? In God's eyes you are special and cherished. Don't you ever believe your life doesn't count. You are more than enough, and God's hand is all over you! You are created by God Himself to live a life of purpose that will glorify Him! You are His!

If you will seek out God's heart for you and read His Word, you will find so much more about who you are than I have just shared here with you. You will find that as you get to know Jesus and allow Him to live and shine through you, you will begin the daily discovery of who you really are meant to be.

Your past, environment, what people say or even your own thoughts about yourself do not determine who you are. Only God determines and seals who you are. You just need to know it, believe it, and walk in it!

Let's work through it...

> ▷ *How can believing this is really who YOU are change your life?*
> ▷ *Go back and REREAD THE SCRIPTURES I listed about who God says you are.*
> ▷ *Write down the ones that He is highlighting to you on index cards and put them in places where you'll see them every day (your room, bathroom mirror, kitchen, car...)*
> ▷ *MEMORIZE the verses you wrote down so that when you're questioning who you are, or you wonder about your life, God's Word will reassure you and give you peace.*

READ THE BOOK OF JOHN IN THE NEW TESTAMENT AND GET TO KNOW JESUS IF YOU DON'T REALLY KNOW HIM OR REACQUAINT YOURSELF WITH HIM. YOU'LL BE PLEASANTLY SURPRISED TO SEE HOW AWESOME HE IS!

5

THE GOAL: DON'T LET ANYONE HOLD YOU BACK

———

The mistakes, the failures, the abuses, all the wrong done to you or that you have done in the past does not define who you are at the very core of your being. This doesn't mean that the past has not influenced you in how you live, react to, or handle life, or that it has not caused you to hurt or experience consequences. But all that has happened to you doesn't *define* the person you've been created to be.

God never intended for you to live in darkness, past or present. He has brought His light to you so that you can clearly see who you truly are and what He has called you to.

You might say, "But the past has affected me in real ways. The past overshadows my present. How can you say that it doesn't define me?" It doesn't have to. That's my point. We'll talk more about this in the next sessions. **What is important, though, is working *through* the past, giving yourself the opportunity to emerge healed, stronger and more confident in who you were created to be.**

You may be someone who did not have a rough past or a negative upbringing, and you may have had a lot of success in life. Maybe life has been comfortable for you. It's been breezy, easy living, but don't be deceived: that still doesn't define who you are. Just because you have had a successful lifestyle so far, is that enough to know who you really were created to be or to live as God intends for you to live?

Life experiences do not equate to your identity

Many base their identity on their life experiences and think that's who they are. But that is not totally true. For example, if one lives in poverty and abuse, then they must be broken and a failure, right? If one lives in wealth and comfort, then they must be whole and successful, right? Wrong! When those things go away, both the bad and the good, who are you then? You must find your identity solely in who God says you are. What He says about you is what really matters. When you discover who He says you are, you'll find that you'll be able to live and thrive in your own authenticity, no matter what circumstances of life you grew up in or did not grow up in.

One encounter with Jesus can change your life!

The story found in Mark 10:46–52(NIV) so inspires me to believe that once you encounter Jesus, you don't have to live in the past anymore, and situations or conditions which have labeled you don't have to anymore. There is life changing power when you encounter Jesus and choose to follow Him! Let's take a look at it:

> Then they came to Jericho. As Jesus and his disciples, together with a large crowd, were leaving the city, a blind man, Bartimaeus (which means "son of Timaeus"), was sitting by the roadside begging. When he heard that it was Jesus of Nazareth, he began to shout, "Jesus, Son of David, have mercy on me!"

> Many rebuked him and told him to be quiet, but he shouted all the more, "Son of David, have mercy on me!"

> Jesus stopped and said, "Call him."

> So they called to the blind man, "Cheer up! On your feet! He's calling you." Throwing his cloak aside, he jumped to his feet and came to Jesus.

"What do you want me to do for you?" Jesus asked him.

The blind man said, "Rabbi, I want to see."

"Go," said Jesus, "your faith has healed you." Immediately he received his sight and followed Jesus along the road. (NIV)

Everyone in town knew Bartimaeus was blind. That's what he was known as—the blind man. When Bartimaeus heard Jesus was in town, he couldn't wait to meet up with Him. When he heard Jesus walking through the crowd, he cried out as loud as he could to get Jesus' attention. You see, he must not have cared what he sounded like or looked like. What was important to him was that Jesus would hear and answer his cry. **Isn't that what we desire? For God to hear our cries and turn towards us?** But while the people around him tried to quiet him down and keep him from going to Jesus, he wouldn't let anyone stop him. He was sick and tired of being the blind beggar everyone knew him as. And he was tired of being blind! He wanted to see!

There needs to come a point when you stop caring about what others think and become so desperate that you'll do everything you can to get to the Savior. What good would it have done Bartimaeus if he had listened to his friends or the people around him to stop crying out? Why *not* keep trying? What if the Savior heard him? He wasn't going to let people stop him. In fact, he was going to cry out even louder! (That's what some of the other Gospels tell about him.) What good will it do you if you submit to what your friends want you to do and you never "go for it" with Jesus? You just might miss out on the biggest miracle of your life!

When Jesus stopped for Bartimaeus and called to him, Bartimaeus threw his cloak aside and ran to Him. He didn't want *anything* hindering him. **He so desperately wanted to be free from anything weighing him down...** He knew what he wanted. He didn't want to be blind anymore. He wanted to see. He wanted his vision to be clear. He wanted a new life. And he went for it. When he did—when he took the risk, by faith—Jesus healed him and gave him a brand new identity, a brand new life.

There's so much more in this story that we can explore, but I shared it to help you see there is hope in Jesus. You don't have to continue being the same person you've been because of what's happened to you or because of how you grew up. You can go to Jesus and have Him change you, but you'll have to step out in faith and take some risks to receive all He has for you.

Let's work through it…

- ▷ *Who in your life are you allowing to hold you back from fully surrendering to Jesus?*
- ▷ *Will you keep pushing through even when others around you try to hold you back?*
- ▷ *What needs to happen for you to take off everything hindering you to run towards the new life and identity God has for you?*
- ▷ *Bartimaeus wanted change, and he went for it. Will you?*

WHAT NEEDS TO HAPPEN FOR YOU TO "GO FOR IT"? (THE CHANGE YOU KNOW YOU NEED TO MAKE)

6

THE GOAL: KNOW THE WHOLE OF YOU

———

Every day as we get ready to go out into our worlds, we look into the mirror, acknowledging and affirming ourselves by what we *do*. We get used to introducing ourselves to others and measuring our successes based off of that. But let's bust that myth! **What you *do* does not define who you *are*. What you do flows out of who you are.**

For example, if you teach, it's because you've been designed with a teaching gift. Therefore, it makes sense to say you are a teacher. If you own a business, it's pretty likely that you are gifted in operating a business and you may then call yourself a business owner. These are things you *do* because of the talents and gifts you've been given. But I want you to think about this carefully: If you define yourself by what you do, then, if you should stop teaching or running a business, who would you be?

So, you're not just a title or a position.

The jobs, titles and positions we take on should not define us. These things are what we do because of how we are designed. I can do many jobs. I can be a mom, a speaker, a writer, a coach, a pastor. These are things I do, but they do not necessarily describe the whole person that I am.

What am I saying here? **It's important to know who you are as a whole person on a deeper level, not just in what you do.**

There's a whole lot more to me than meets the eye! There's a lot more to me that many people around me may or may not know about me. For example: I am a compassionate, confident and hard-working woman. I am also a very hands-on person and can be a perfectionist at times. I have a love for teenagers and the underdog. I am a strong person who usually takes charge, but I also feel inadequate in many areas and need someone to hold my hand at times. I am quick to apologize, and I hate conflict. I don't hold a grudge, but I guard my heart in relationships. I don't like getting hurt. That's kind of interesting to find out about a person, isn't it? Am I helping you to see a bigger picture of myself? A more 'whole' person than meets the eye?

I have a set of core values I live my life by, and I try not to compromise them in my everyday decision-making. I have a strong Christian faith that I'm hopefully growing in every day. As I grow in my relationship with the Lord and in my other relationships, I believe I know what I will tolerate and what I won't. I believe I have a sound mind, so I don't have to operate from confusion or chaos. *Et cetera, et cetera.*

Do you see where I want to take you? These are just examples of knowing who I *am* based on who God made me to be and not just based on what I *do*.

It's not as though you need to tell the world who you are at this level, but you need to grasp and acknowledge the kind of person that you are so you don't just become a title or someone filling a position in life. You are actually someone with substance and quality and value. You are a person worth getting to know—inside and out!

We are not just a teacher, a business owner, a doctor, or a mother. We are much more than meets the eye. We have thoughts, opinions, convictions. We have qualities that too often get overlooked or forgotten because we're too busy *doing* and not taking the time to *be*. That's where I believe we miss it. There's so much about us that is powerful and beautiful as God made us, but we give that all up to adopt the idea that what we *do* is more important or impressive than who we *are*.

We must be careful to understand the difference, so that no matter what we do or stop doing in life, we will stay true to our authentic selves and never lose sight of the unique and powerful people God designed us to be.

When did it all become so complicated?

Could it be that the process of simply saying who you are has become complicated? Complicated, perhaps, because many voices—those of society, social media, peer groups, family, political correctness, even church or religion—are influencing you more than you think? **Are these voices and their expectations of you causing you to feel the need to hide, lie, exaggerate or protect yourself against their opinions or views of who you are or who you should be?** Do you feel yourself getting lost about who you really are?

These questions deserve your honest answer. If you don't really know how to introduce yourself or what you think of yourself, what does living life look like for you? Can you truly live life authentically and to the fullest?

Shut out the voices. All of them.

Look in the mirror of God's word and ask yourself, "Who am I? Who am I, *really*? What am I all about?" Listen in to the one voice that truly matters—the voice of your Creator who knows you better than you know yourself. **Shut out the voices (yes, all of them) until you can clearly hear His voice.** Can you hear it? Ask: "Who does GOD say I am?" When you do, you will experience life-changing answers.

Nothing more than feelings...

You can't define yourself from the perspective of how you *feel*. What you feel about yourself is not who you are or what makes you. Feelings are not always based on truth. Truth sets us free, not feelings. You might feel like a failure, but are you a failure? No! You might have failed at doing something, but that does not make you a failure. **You need to be aware of what you allow your feelings to determine so that you operate from truth and not feelings.** Get off the feelings rollercoaster!

Don't stop short just because you think all is well

You might be saying, "Well, my life isn't that bad. I like myself. I'm comfortable with who I am. I don't think I need to think that deeply about it." That's great! But let me challenge you—are you satisfied? Are you satisfied with where you are in your relationship with God? Are you satisfied with what He's done for you in the past, but you're not really going for all He has for you in the future? Do you know for sure that what you have to share with people today is all you've got to tell? Have you tapped out on the limits of all God has called you to be? Don't get too comfortable or settle into the obvious of who you are. **Dig deeper, push through, and maybe you'll discover you're more of a gem than you thought!**

I believe it's time to get to know yourself deep down in your heart where pain, victories, regrets and hope exist, where faith resides, strength is built, and your character is shaped through the highs and lows of life. It's time to reach in, get rid of all that's not supposed to be there, and pull out all that's supposed to rise and shine out of you. There is so much about you and in you that God wants to help you discover.

I pray that in the following chapters, the question of your true identity and all God has called you to will be answered. In the meantime, stop seeing yourself from your past, whether it was negative or positive. Experiences in and of themselves don't define you. The truth of who God says you are defines you.

Wherever you've come from in life or wherever you're at now, I challenge you to allow Holy Spirit to shine His light on your thoughts, your heart, your talk, your walk and all that you think you are (or aren't). You'll discover how much more there is to you.

Let's work through it...

▷   *Have you been defining yourself as what you do?*

▷   *What voices have you been listening to that you may have allowed to define you?*

▷   *What life experience(s) can you point to that you may have allowed to define you?*

▷   *How can you begin to know yourself at a "whole" level?*

WHAT ARE SOME OF THE DEEPER THINGS IN YOU THAT NEED TO SHINE?

7

THE GOAL: CHOOSE TO BE HIS

———

There's such a longing in each of our hearts to belong. When one doesn't feel like he or she belongs, it can create a lifetime of identity crisis, trauma, abandonment and rejection issues. But in this session, I'm here to tell you that you *do* belong and that there is a place in a special family that is reserved just for you! And you will always be welcome in it! But before I continue on with that, I want to tell you about a TV show that I really enjoy watching. Some of you may know it: It's about family members finding each other after being separated from their loved ones at birth.

Family is one of the most powerful things God created, but sadly, many don't know the joys of being in a healthy and stable one. And many don't experience the positive impact of its purpose. *Family* doesn't always paint a positive picture. The family unit in our society has been broken and many find themselves separated from those who were supposed to love them and care for them. Considering God created us to have loving, healthy, thriving relationships with our family, that is a sad fact. On the show, people reconnect with biological parents, children or siblings with whom they've lost contact. The strong, deep desires of those who have been adopted or who gave babies up for adoption years ago to find each other always amazes me. The deep need some have to know who they belong to, where their roots are, what family they could have called their very own can become almost unbearable to those who don't have the answers. When they find out, the knowledge suddenly brings them a sense of relief, clarity, and a peace they can't explain. **It gives them a sense of hope, an anchoring to something more solid than themselves. It's like they've found the missing piece to a puzzle.**

I've watched all of the people on the show's episodes express exactly this truth which applies to us all: *We were created to belong.* ***You* were created to belong.** Everyone yearns to belong to someone or something and we hope that sense of belonging will give us meaning. It's just the way we were made. On the show, before the subjects meet their birth families, they often feel like they don't really belong to anyone.

Knowing your biological family or where you come from is valuable information. It can provide answers to questions in many areas of life. There's much good that can come out of knowing our biological roots, but even in knowing that, we have to be careful that that information isn't what gives our life its *true* meaning.

We get to meet our Father and our other family members!

I believe life takes on true meaning when we respond to the invitation to become children of God. What an awesome privilege that is! When we accept Jesus Christ as our personal Savior, we come into relationship with God as our *Father*. **He not only is our Creator, but He becomes our Father who welcomes us into His family.** He provides a family for us to belong to. And not just for a time here on earth, but for all of eternity. Can you imagine belonging to a family whose only goal is to love and to be loved? A family where hope, peace and true joy can be found? Can you imagine yourself in a family who accepts each other and know how to love because the Father of that family is the very essence and definition of love?

Our enemy, the devil, would want nothing more than to cause us to feel abandoned, alone and as orphans, without the true love of a Father, without the true encouragement of a family. But God saw to it that we would have the opportunity to enjoy the personal love of a Father and His family through His Son, Jesus Christ.

When we find our place in God's family, we find a whole new meaning. We are no longer orphans. We no longer have to be by ourselves, trying to figure life out. **We get to live with purpose, fulfilling the will of our Father.** We get to love Him by worshiping Him with our new family of God. We get to love others by serving them and using our gifts to impact our world together. When we become children of God, we get to live life to the fullest because our Father is life itself!

Our Father God will never forsake us

We are cared for by Him. He watches over us like a doting father. He never leaves us or forsakes us. He is our Protector, Provider, Comforter, Friend, and so much more. When we are adopted into His love, His blessings for us are endless and His unconditional love sustains us more than anything ever could. **We belong to Him and no one or nothing can ever take Him away from us!**

Who we are related to and the area we come from on this earth doesn't even compare to having God as our Father and belonging to Him. Where we come from on this earth doesn't give the true meaning of our existence. We have meaning because God Himself gives us meaning. If we let Him, God will use where we come from to serve His good purposes in our lives. Romans 8:28 says, "And we know that God causes everything to work together for the good of those who love God and are called according to his purpose for them" (NLT).

Biological likeness

Many on the TV show I mentioned who search for their birth parents or siblings are curious to know who they *look* like. Isn't that interesting? They figure if they *look* like someone, then they must *belong* to that someone. When they are finally reunited with their birth families, that is such a focal point—who they look like.

Post-episode follow-ups of these reunions show how the families fare together after they reunited. It's often sad to learn that although some of the biological family members may have discovered that they look alike, they may have been nothing alike in personality. Their morals, work ethics, mindsets or belief systems are frequently so different that they find it challenging to build healthy, solid relationships. **Just because people look alike and share the same genes does not mean they share the things and values that are most important to them.**

When we choose to be adopted by God, we also begin the journey to not only belong to Him but also to look like Him, spiritually. We begin to desire to align our lifestyle with what He looks like, outwardly expressing it through His fruit that we bear (Galatians 5:21 & 22). (I speak more on this in the sessions to come.)

Adoption is being chosen

Adoption is a blessed and special thing. When a family chooses to adopt a child into their family, they are choosing to welcome that child, to care for him or her and to provide all things that child needs to live and grow healthy. That's what happens when we choose to belong to God and allow Him to adopt us as His very own. He makes sure we are provided for and cared for that we might grow up in Him, not lacking in anything. God always intended for us to be with Him, but sin came and separated us from Him. I'm so thankful that Jesus Christ came to redeem us back into the family that we were originally created to be in!

Are you reborn of God?

The term *reborn* has a greater meaning when we understand that we don't have to be a child of the evil nature anymore. **To be reborn of His spirit is the most important choice God gave us so that we might become one of His.**

Here are some scriptures from the Father's heart that welcome us into His family.

> For those who are led by the Spirit of God are the children of God. The Spirit you received does not make you slaves, so that you live in fear again; rather, the Spirit you received brought about your

adoption to sonship. And by him we cry, "Abba, Father." The Spirit himself testifies with our spirit that we are God's children. (Romans 8:14–16 NIV)

"And I will be a father to you, And you shall be sons and daughters to Me," Says the Lord Almighty. (2 Corinthians 6:18 NASB)

Therefore you are no longer a slave, but a son; and if a son, then an heir through God. (Galatians 4:7 NASB)

But as many as received Him, to them He gave the right to become children of God, even to those who believe in His name... (John 1:12 NASB)

God desires that you be His very own, and He has invited you to be a part of His family from the very beginning of your creation, but He leaves that choice to you. I pray that you said *Yes!* to being adopted into the circle of His everlasting love!

Let's work through it...

His love is so great for you that He gave you the free will to choose Him and to belong to Him forever.

- ▷ *How important is it for you to feel as though you belong to someone? And why?*
- ▷ *In what areas have you in the past or may you now be struggling with belonging? To God? To a family of believers?*
- ▷ *How do you know you belong to the Father?*
- ▷ *Are you part of His family? What does that look like for you? If not yet, what can you do about this?*
- ▷ *Can you say you look like your Heavenly Father? How so?*

8

THE GOAL: BUST THE MYTHS—YOU ARE NOT YOUR MOTHER OR FATHER

———

The words quickly and easily fly out of your mouth, and it hits you: you have become your mother! You sound like her. You react like her, so you must be just like her. Small things like this, or perhaps even more significant happenings, may cause you to believe that you are becoming an exact replica of your mom or dad. The fact of the matter is…

You are NOT your mother! You are NOT your father! You may *feel* like your mother or your father, but you are not. You may *wish* you were like your mother or your father, but you never can be them. You may wish to *never* be like your mother or father, but worry that you can't get away from being like them. You might think: *I was born to be just like them.*

But you are not. You may pick up some habits or patterns of theirs over the years, or even come under the influence of some spirits they carry, but you are NOT them! *(This is discussed more in detail in the session dealing with generational curses).*

Don't be tempted to say, "I'm just like my mother," or "I'm a workaholic like my dad was," or "My mom was an addict, so I'm probably going to be one too."

Never and nowhere in God's Word does it say that you have been made in the image of your earthly mother or father or that whatever they're like automatically gets passed on to you. Now, if you've had a great mom or dad and you aspire to honor them by following their godly, inspiring example of their good character they modeled for you, then that's great! Keep living in and applying all of the good they imparted into you and pass those things along to your own children.

Please hear me: Psalm 139 doesn't say your mom or your dad formed you in your mother's womb. It never says your mom or dad fashioned all your days for you and wrote every one of them in their book for you. Take a look—this is King David talking to God about creating him in the womb:

> You formed my innermost being, shaping my delicate inside
> and my intricate outside,
> and wove them all together in my mother's womb.
> I thank you, God, for making me so mysteriously complex!
> Everything you do is marvelously breathtaking.
> It simply amazes me to think about it!
> How thoroughly you know me, LORD!
> You even formed every bone in my body
> when you created me in the secret place,
> carefully, skillfully shaping me from nothing to something.
> You saw who you created me to be before I became me!
> Before I'd ever seen the light of day,
> the number of days you planned for me
> were already recorded in your book. (Psalm 139:13–16 TPT)

Just as God used David to pen these words for himself, it is an important message for each of us as well. It is a personal message from God to you that you may know without a doubt that GOD formed you, fashioned you, and has a plan for your life. **Yes, your earthly mother gave birth to you, but she didn't have the power within her to create who you are. Only God could do that.** A woman and a man were involved in a physical, sexual union and God used that physical foundation and created you.

Whether you've had a great childhood and great parents, whether you were planned or unplanned, whether you were born out of a rape or from an unexpected situation, GOD wanted you and used all of what happened to form you and love you from that place. **God is love, and so you were created by love itself!** Right from the get-go, you were loved! No one else had the power to make you, and no one else has the power today to make you!

The behavior and patterns you may have picked up from your parents are just that. They are things that you *picked up* and learned from the way they say things, handle things, react to things. Those are *their* behaviors that you may have owned as part of who you are, but they are not what makes *you*. If you assess how you, the real you, handles things and says things and responds to things, is it *exactly* the way that your mother or father does? Based on your values (which we'll explore more later on), your beliefs, your personality and what you know of yourself, how different are you from them? If you say that you are indeed exactly like them, I want to challenge you to keep reading with the understanding that God made you unique after all.

How much power are you giving to your genes?

Just because you share the same DNA with your parents does not mean that you get the permission to act as they do, to think as they do, to live as they do. Many people I've counseled and coached prefer to lean on excuses for why they can't change their negative behaviors or their course of life because their mom or dad acted, thought or lived that way, and that is their cross to bear, too! There are people sabotaging their own lives because they are living this lie. Therefore, in their minds, there is no hope of changing or of being different than their parent(s).

Are we going to allow our 'genes' or acquired behavior patterns from our mothers and fathers to dictate how we live our own lives? Or are we going to take responsibility for our own behaviors and actions in order to change for the better? Is it difficult to change? Yes, it can be, but with effort, renewed thinking, and God's help, it is possible.

Renewing your mind takes discipline. Daily effort is required to change the way you think and the way you speak. But it is possible! For some, it's easier to blame your failures or your habits on the lie that you're "just like good ol' mom and dad." If that's how you think, it's time to kick that lie to the curb! Begin to do things differently. Be aware of the choices you make, the people you hang around with, the words that you speak. Be aware of your thought pattern and your moods. Be aware and align yourself with what the Word of God says you are.

> Do not merely listen to the word, and so deceive yourselves. Do what it says. (James 1:22 NIV)

So, no more excuses to not be the best you God created *you* to be! If you want to move forward in your life you cannot continue using this as your excuse. **Whatever impact or influence your parents have had on you, you were never meant to *be* them.**

Time to come out of that shadow and into the light God has called you into!

Identity crisis and Hollywood

We pick up and own a lot of behaviors and patterns that are not our own. Most are probably from our mother or father, but other outside influences mess with who we are and how we live out our lives. Let's look at a couple.

Have you noticed we seem to be in an *identity crisis* these days? We are concerned with questions like these:

Who do I look like? Who do I act like? Who do I please? Who needs me to be perfect? Who is disappointed in me? How did I get like this?

Over and over, I see people discredit themselves, compare themselves, and come up feeling short. Over and over again, I see people struggling with confusion because someone told them *that's* who they are, *that's* how they're supposed to behave and *that's* where they belong. And a lot of the time, **they are being fed lies to serve someone else's agenda.**

Society and media convince and condition us to see ourselves as something other than who and what *God* originally designed us to be. This is a tactic of Satan's we need to expose and demolish in our lives immediately. The enemy uses what we have allowed—TV, movies, magazines, social media, and yes, even people we idolize—to create a false truth about ourselves, to turn lies into perceived reality.

When you believe that you can be anything that you want to be *outside of God's will* for you, you will eventually experience emptiness, chaos, frustration and regret. Why? Because God made you and knows you from the inside out. He knows who you are supposed to be. He knows what He's put inside of you, and living outside of that truth will not bring you true happiness and peace. If you know the mind of Christ for you, you will know who you are to be and how He wants you to live.

How can you stop living under their influence?

> Beloved friends, what should be our proper response to God's marvelous mercies? I encourage you to surrender yourselves to God to be his sacred, living sacrifices. And live in holiness, experiencing all that delights his heart. For this becomes your genuine expression of worship.
>
> Stop imitating the ideals and opinions of the culture around you, but be inwardly transformed by the Holy Spirit through a total reformation of how you think. This will empower you to discern God's will as you live a beautiful life, satisfying and perfect in his eyes. (Romans 12:1–2 TPT)

There it is right there! Surrender to God. Live in holiness. What does that mean? To live in holiness is to live a life that is set apart for God. It's doing things His way and not giving in to the pressure of doing things "their" way. It's following His ways and walking in faith and trusting where God is taking you. It's receiving what His thoughts are about you. Surrendering is making each choice according to what His Word says. **We complicate it, but it doesn't have to be complicated. God maps it all out for us in His Word. It's up to us to choose to live by it.**

Stop imitating the world and culture around you. Stop being influenced by ungodly influences. The enemy devises schemes against you, and that's one of his lying ones! Just because you may admire an actor or an athlete doesn't mean they have the authority to change you or make you something other than God's plan for you. But you give them that authority when you change who you really are to try to meet fantasy ideals and standards they put out there. News flash: They don't even know you exist!

During my years of youth pastoring, I've found many young people succumb to lies from Hollywood or social media in regards to body image, talent and morals (or lack thereof). And just to be popular or liked, many gave their power over to these idols who really don't even exist in their lives but are only present via screens and imagination. So sad… It needs to stop if you're going to live a life worthy of the calling and love of God. You can be all God has designed for you to be, and that is something more amazing than you could possibly imagine. With the power of Holy Spirit working in you, you can be transformed in your thinking. When your life is aligned with God's ways, you will not experience confusion: rather, you will know God's will and live a fulfilled life in Him.

You've got to choose

You've been given the truth of who you are in God through His Word to you. The world becomes small when you see yourself only as your parents or others see you, or who they say you are. Your life becomes limited and miserable when you try to live to the standards of the Hollywood images staring back at you from magazines or movies or social media. That becomes a dangerous place to live from.

Who or what is shaping your self-image? Is it fantasy? Is it wishful thinking to become like your favorite celebrity or athlete? Is it the high and mighty dollar that's dictated your worth or lack of?

If you stop saying and believing things such as: "I'm just like my mother," or "I'm just like my father," or "I wish I looked like such-and-such a celebrity or such-and-such an athlete or singer," and start saying, "I am beautiful inside and out!", "I have so much to give!", "I am full of light and life, just like Jesus!", "I am strong with the strength of God's power in me, and I can get through this!" or "I will not fear because my Father in Heaven has not deposited in me a spirit of fear, but of love, power and a sound mind," how different do you think your life would be? How powerful, purposed and victorious would you be? Speaking His truth will begin to set you free!

> The tongue has the power of life and death, and those who love it will eat its fruit. (Proverbs 18:21 NIV)

Begin to believe who God says you are and that you belong to your heavenly Father. Speak it over yourself daily, and watch your life take on new meaning and joy in all you do!

I pray that you would find peace and contentment in learning to love yourself, body, soul and spirit without comparing yourself to airbrushed Hollywood. Nor would you compare yourself to athletes who may *seem* to have it all together. The money, the fame, the game… it's all temporary. You may think you are or should be more like your parents, but really, what life is God calling you to? Who is He calling you to be? **You have all you need in Christ. That's not meant to be just another cliché, but rather a truth that will bring you freedom and joy if you will walk in it.** If you truly know Jesus, you know what I'm talking about. In Him is found true identity. In Him is found contentment with who you are. Every day you get to grow to look more like Him and that is part of our purpose here.

So, shake off the pressure to be someone else and embrace and enjoy who God has called you to be!

Let's work through it…

Never anywhere in the Bible will you find that God created us in our earthly father or mother's image! Never. Nowhere. It only says that we were created in HIS image (Genesis 1:26 & 27).

> ▷ *If you began to see yourself as created in the image of God, how might your life change?*
> ▷ *What needs to happen in order for you to stop believing you are not your mother or your father?*
> ▷ *How destructive do you believe is it to pattern your life on what Hollywood or this world tells you is THE standard by which you need to live by to succeed or be accepted?*

We must always remember that no outside person, environment, atmosphere or situation has the power to determine who God made us to be on the inside.

HAVE YOU GIVEN POWER TO SOMEONE ELSE TO DETERMINE WHO YOU NEED TO BE? HOW CAN YOU BREAK FROM THAT AND GIVE THAT POWER OVER TO GOD WHO CREATED YOU?

SECTION 2

The Power of
Your Words

Goals:

- ▶ Speak life
- ▶ Become aware of what you *do* know

GET OFF THE THRONE

9

THE GOAL: SPEAK LIFE

———

"Excuse me, but what did you say?"

Words have the power to create your life.

Maybe you've spoken some NEGATIVE WORDS over yourself, or maybe you've allowed people in your life to speak words over (or at) you that have affected the way you do life. I mean words like these: *won't, can't, never will, failure, amount to nothing, it's beyond you, you're too dumb, you'll never last, you won't finish, it's too hard, you're not cut out for that, it's impossible, who do you think you are, you don't have what it takes,* etc…

You may not realize that words spoken over and over into your life have formed the life you live—or at least a part of it. Words can create your belief system. Think about this for a minute. Words that come out of your mouth are words you usually follow through with. If you continually speak negative words over yourself or you continuously allow others to speak them at you, you will begin to believe them (at least subconsciously), and those words get into your soul (your mind, your emotions, your will) and into your spirit. You will find yourself fulfilling them and living by them. You'll notice all the flaws and all the imperfections, and then you'll begin to magnify them. You may begin to walk around in a self-conscious manner, and your confidence may shrink down to next to nothing. Everything you do can be affected by negative words you absorb.

For example: If you continuously say to yourself, "I wasn't born smart," you'll always believe it and you'll never try something that may require extra effort or change on your part. You'll always and only do what you're most comfortable with; stick to things that you're familiar with; believe that anything outside of your self-made box is impossible and unattainable. That's what it means in Proverbs 18:21—you will "eat the fruit" of the words you speak.

When you speak lies, doubt and evil, you speak the devil's language. You give him permission to come in and work so that those words establish his schemes and plans in your life.

> He has nothing to do with the truth, because there is no truth in him. When he lies, he speaks out of his own character, for he is a liar and the father of lies. (John 8:44 ESV)

Do not listen to the words and the lies the enemy whispers in your ear. Do not allow his foul words to defile you and cause you to live outside God's will for you. **Call the enemy out on it and refuse to allow any more of his words to influence or overtake you.**

Speaking the devil's language and words create an atmosphere filled with oppression, darkness, hopelessness and defeat. He is a liar, as Jesus calls him, so stop speaking his words over your life!

Remember: the tongue holds the power of life and death (Proverbs 18:21).

Your words create

In the beginning, in Genesis chapter 1, we see that God *said* these words: "'Let there be light', and there was light" (NASB). Is light/day still happening in our world today? Yes! That's because God spoke it into existence, and unless He retracts His words, we will continue to have light/day! God spoke it, and it happened! Such power in His words! Take note! Throughout that chapter, you will see that God *said* many things and spoke those things into existence, thus creating the Earth.

So think about this: if you and I are made in His image and He has the power which allows His words to create, then I believe you and I have that ability, too. If you don't believe this, I challenge you to take a very close look at your life right now. What do you see? Can you honestly say that your words have not affected how you're living today and may have created the environment or circumstances/consequences around you? I say this, the kind of life you're living may be because of the words you've spoken or keep speaking to create it! Reflect on that and see if there just might be some truth to that.

The Word of God has a lot to say about your tongue. It is a small body part, but wow! It can bring about destruction, or it can bring healing and life. Let's take a look at some scriptures that talk about this.

Death and life are in the power of the tongue,
And those who love it will eat its fruit. (Proverbs 18:21 NKJV)

Whoever would love life
and see good days
must keep their tongue from evil
and their lips from deceitful speech. (1 Peter 3:10 NIV)

The soothing tongue is a tree of life,
but a perverse tongue crushes the spirit. (Proverbs 15:4 NIV)

The words of the reckless pierce like swords,
but the tongue of the wise brings healing. (Proverbs 12:18 NIV)

Likewise, the tongue is a small part of the body, but it makes great boasts. Consider what a great forest is set on fire by a small spark. The tongue also is a fire, a world of evil among the parts of the body. It corrupts the whole body, sets the whole course of one's life on fire, and is itself set on fire by hell.

All kinds of animals, birds, reptiles and sea creatures are being tamed and have been tamed by mankind, but no human being can tame the tongue. It is a restless evil, full of deadly poison.

With the tongue we praise our Lord and Father, and with it we curse human beings, who have been made in God's likeness. Out of the same mouth come praise and cursing. My brothers and sisters, this should not be. Can both fresh water and salt water flow from the same spring? My brothers and sisters, can a fig tree bear olives, or a grapevine bear figs? Neither can a salt spring produce fresh water. (James 3:5–12 NIV)

Those verses on what God has to say about your tongue are self-explanatory. The words you speak can create situations in your life for the good or bad. **Your own words reflecting negativity or agreeing with the lies of the enemy can sabotage your destiny.** Your words, aligned with lies, can ruin your relationships and cause unnecessary pain. I could go on about the destruction your words can cause, but I think you get the picture.

On the other hand, your words can bring life and healing to you and to situations around you. What you say can affect your relationships and bring hope and love to others. **Speaking God's words, positive words over your life or others' lives causes your purpose and destiny to take shape.** They are powerful to eradicate the lies and to create peace and a sense of well-being. When you speak words that are life-giving, you have the power to change your ways.

Speaking God's Word over your life

What you speak over who God has called you to be and what God has called you to do makes a huge difference. **You can speak God's word and promises over yourself and your destiny and watch God honor it, or you can speak evil and lies over your life and watch the devil influence it.**

You may not have heard it put like this before, but it's true. Look at the power of God's words…

As the rain and the snow
   come down from heaven,

and do not return to it
    without watering the earth
and making it bud and flourish
    so that it yields seed for the sower and bread for the eater,
so is my word that goes out from my mouth:
    It will not return to me empty,
but will accomplish what I desire
    and achieve the purpose for which I sent it. (Isaiah 55:10–
    11 NIV)

This is a powerful truth that has the power to change your life forever.

When you speak *God's words*, they do not return to Him empty. He uses His word to accomplish His desires. Did you get that? When you speak *God's* promises and His word to your situations and over your life, He is faithful to accomplish them! In whatever situation you're facing, seek out what GOD says about it and then pray that over it instead of your own words.

For example: If you lost your job, instead of speaking defeat and speaking complaints and negativity, seek out what God's word says about it. For example, in Matthew 6, you'll find that God says He provides much more for you than he provides for a bird of the air! Take that promise from God and speak His truth over your job situation. God's Word will accomplish His own perfect will over our situations as we pray it back to Him. It doesn't return to Him void!

That's why it is important to know the Word of God. It is crucial to know what He says about you and what He provides for you through His Word.

How can you know this is true?

- Read the Word of God.
- Believe the Word of God.
- Speak the Word of God.
- Watch the Word of God bring you hope and victory!

Be aware of what comes out of your mouth. Believe that what you speak, you are creating! Do you want to create a place for the Holy Spirit to reside? Do you want to live in love, hope, peace and joy? Then speak God's words that only He can establish in you.

Let's work through it…

God's Word is serious about how we use our tongue. Take some time and think about the words you speak over yourself and over others.

 ▷ *What words do I usually speak (or think) over myself? Do the words I speak bring death or life?*
 ▷ *What needs to happen to change the way I speak over myself and to others?*
 ▷ *Do I just skim over the Word of God, or do I know what it actually says so that I might speak His truth?*

You might want to pray…

GOD, I REPENT OF ALL THE NEGATIVE WORDS AND DECLARATIONS I'VE MADE OVER MYSELF OVER THE YEARS. I REJECT ALL THE NEGATIVE WORDS THAT WERE SPOKEN OVER ME AND AT ME BY OTHERS THAT I'VE RECEIVED AS TRUTH. THOSE WORDS WERE LIES AND NOT TRUTH. I REJECT THEM, AND I DON'T BELIEVE THEM ANYMORE. I ALSO REPENT FOR SPEAKING LIES OVER WHAT YOU HAVE FOR ME, GOD. I REPENT FOR NOT BELIEVING THAT WITH YOU, I CAN DO ALL THINGS, THAT I AM WHO YOU SAY I AM AND THAT WHAT YOU PLANNED FOR MY LIFE IS POSSIBLE! GOD FORGIVE ME FOR LIMITING MYSELF AND FOR LIMITING YOU WORKING IN MY LIFE. FORGIVE ME FOR ALL THE NEGATIVE WORDS THAT I HAVE SPOKEN OVER OTHERS. HELP ME TO SPEAK LIFE OVER THEM. MAKE ALL THINGS NEW, LORD. HELP ME TO CONTROL THE WORDS I SPEAK AND HELP ME TO CREATE LIFE WITH MY TONGUE. IN JESUS' NAME I PRAY THIS. AMEN.

10

THE GOAL: BECOMING AWARE OF WHAT YOU DO KNOW…

———

Many get "stuck" because they keep telling themselves they don't know what to do about _____ (fill in the blank).

The very words "I don't know" can bring on insecurities, anxieties, stress and even at times can leave you feeling hopeless or helpless. So, how's repeatedly saying "I don't know" working out for you? It probably isn't. As long as you keep believing, thinking and speaking out "I don't know" over both big and small things of your life, you will never be able to fully move forward into the next decision, phase or even the next step in life. As long as you keep yourself in an "I don't know" attitude, and practically make not knowing your belief system, it will overpower all of what you actually do know. Your thinking won't be clear, and your choices and decisions will be based on the negative and not on the positive. That allows the negative to be a stronger force in your life than the positive that God designed for you to live in.

I want to challenge what you may have conditioned yourself to believe. **Flip the statement "I don't know" and instead ask yourself the question, "What _do_ I know?"** Honestly answer it. What _do_ you know about _____ (fill in the blank)?

Now, say it or write it: "I know _____."

You'll probably find you can make many *I know* statements. When you take the time to become aware of and discover what you actually *do* know, a whole new perspective opens up that will cause you to have the peace and hope you need to get you moving forward. **What you *do* know will begin to bring clarity.** It will begin to put an affirmative spin on helping you clearly see the next step to take. What you DO know will bring you closer to making the next choice, and the next, and the next… until you walk with certainty and confidence.

You will be surprised at how much you really *do* know about the situation or about yourself or about what you need to be doing. You will also be surprised at how much you do know of what GOD is saying about the situation! You can KNOW what HE says about every single thing you're going through! What is GOD saying about your job? Your relationships? Your school or career? What is GOD saying about your fears, anxiety, pain or success? How can you know what He says about it? **Search His word if you don't know, and then begin to apply what you DO know! It is life-changing!**

So, flip that negative statement around and ask yourself, "What *do* I know?" You will see how things could change for the better! When you acknowledge what you do know it will be your launching pad for making the next decision and the next and the next.

Let's work through it…

- ▷ *In what areas or thoughts are you struggling with regarding knowing what to do?*
- ▷ *What are some things you may need to do to be more positive and confident in the issues you are dealing with?*
- ▷ *Write down what you DO know about your situation and let that become the building block for taking the next step.*

HOW COULD THE QUESTION "WHAT DO I KNOW?" BENEFIT THE WAY YOU LIVE YOUR LIFE FROM HERE ON?

11

THE GOAL: GET OFF THE THRONE

———

You may have heard of *inner vows*. I had never heard of them until I heard Pastor Jimmy Evans of Gateway Church in Southlake, Texas, speak about them, and I was totally floored! I had never heard such revelation before. As I began to apply the idea of inner vows to my own life and as I began sharing the idea with others, I began to see breakthroughs in my life and in the lives of many of my clients.

Before I share more about what I believe God has shown me about inner vows, consider the following statements adapted and excerpted from Jimmy Evans' book, *When Life Hurts*. It offers incredible insight for the beginning of anyone's healing and freedom journey.

> *Wounds must be tended. A cut must be cleaned out and protected to avoid infection. We douse injuries in alcohol and antibiotic. We apply bandages to help wounds heal.*
>
> *It's much harder to deal with inner wounds. That pain may be just as destructive, but because we can't always see the injury, we don't know how to treat it. Often we ignore the wound and pretend it doesn't exist. That's a mistake. The wound festers. An infection spreads, and before we know it, this toxic emotional pain has scarred and damaged us. So instead of treating the wound, we make inner vows to help us avoid further pain. These are unhealthy promises we make to comfort ourselves in times of frustration or difficulty:*

No one will ever treat me like that again.

I'll never let myself be poor.

I'll never let anyone break my heart like that again.

Inner vows cause us to overreact, and they can become the guiding force of our lives. They don't just undermine our emotional stability. They also damage our relationships—including our relationship with God—and cause us to act out in unhealthy, irrational ways. Inner vows are sinful. They create in us a heart of stone. But through the prophet Ezekiel, God tells us this: "I will give you a new heart and put a new spirit in you; I will remove from you your heart of stone and give you a heart of flesh" (Ezek. 36:26 NIV). God can remove the hardness from our hearts if we allow Him. God promises a new heart and a new spirit. He promises freedom. We find it when we surrender our inner vows to God. We give Him complete and total access to those painful parts of ourselves and ask Him to perform a miracle in our heart and spirit.

This is a great revelation of how inner vows are made. **How we deal with or don't deal with our wounds can cause us to make inner vows that keep us living bound up on the inside.**

Is God sitting on the throne of your heart, or are you?

For example, if you made an inner vow and said, "I will never be poor again," what you're really saying is this: "*I* will make sure that *I* always have money and that *I* control that area in my life. *I* won't let anyone stop me from having money. *I* will decide where *I* give and how much, and *I* will work as hard as *I* need to so that *I* will always have lots of money!"

Who is sitting on the throne of that area of finances? There isn't anything inherently wrong with working hard and making lots of money. But that's not the issue in this inner vow. The issue is that *I* (you) is sitting on that throne and acting as king over it. **And as long as you are king over that area, there is no room for God to be King over it.**

If God wants to move you to another career, or He wants you to give here or there, you may get defensive, stubborn, selfish and fearful. If you do, He won't be able to work out His plans for that area of your life because you've left no room for Him there. It would be hard for you to trust Him and to obey Him in this area. And if you can't trust Him and obey Him, He won't be able to work it out.

You may have made an inner vow that no one will ever hurt you again. You will make sure no man (or woman) will ever be able to get close to you again. For example, you're single and you really want to get married, but when that certain person God may have provided to be your spouse comes along, you feel he or she is so great—almost perfect in every way—but there's just *something* wrong. You can't figure out why, but you can't seem to get close. It feels like there's a barrier.

Why? Perhaps the inner vow—that you would never let anyone close to you again—is in charge of your heart. Did you make vows from a place of woundedness, maybe in anger and pain? If you did, you sit on your heart as king. Until you dethrone yourself, God cannot be King.

You can't have an inner vow established and have God's blessings in that area at the same time. You and God cannot both be King!

As long as you are on the throne of that area, you cannot receive the person God has provided for you. Your inner vow of never getting hurt again, never giving your heart to someone will keep that person far from you. How can this be? Because the inner vow you made is set in stone, so to speak. (Remember the verse about having a heart of stone?) It will be respected until you break it.

How can an inner vow be respected?

God is a covenant-making God. He made covenants with His people in the Old Testament, and Jesus made a covenant with His followers in the New Testament before He went to the cross. When He took communion with His disciples, He was establishing His covenant between them. Communion symbolized the breaking of the body of

Christ and the shedding of His blood for us. It was the greatest and ultimate sacrifice made for man to be able to enter into true covenant and lasting fellowship with God.

God makes covenants to keep them. He does not take vows or covenants lightly. Jesus made a covenant with us with His very own blood. **Covenants are a serious thing! They bind. They seal. They're supposed to be forever.**

Ecclesiastes gives a glimpse of how serious God is about making vows.

> Do not be quick with your mouth,
>   do not be hasty in your heart
>   to utter anything before God.
> God is in heaven
>   and you are on earth,
>   so let your words be few.
> A dream comes when there are many cares,
>   and many words mark the speech of a fool.

When you make a vow to God, do not delay fulfilling it. He has no pleasure in fools; fulfill your vow. It is better not to make a vow than to make one and not fulfill it. Do not let your mouth lead you into sin. And do not protest to the temple messenger, "My vow was a mistake." Why should God be angry at what you say and destroy the work of your hands? Much dreaming and many words are meaningless. Therefore fear God. (Ecclesiastes 5:2–7 NIV)

Wow! We must be careful what we say; we must be careful what we vow. Do you see how seriously God takes vows? Do you see that once He establishes a vow, He respects it? Whether we think a vow is a good one or a bad one, when it is established, it activates its intent. In other words, it produces its fruit in your life (just like the power of your words can). **And because of our hastiness in making vows that are not godly, we end up reaping the consequences of that.** As we studied earlier, our words create. In a negative sense, our words can create a barrier to the blessings of God. When our hearts are wounded, our words can either bring healing or death. If our wounded soul (mind, emotions and will) agrees with our words, we will be bound to that feeling or decision until we speak truth and life over it.

Breaking that inner vow

Because God is just, He respects the establishment of vows. So even if a vow is not established on godliness, He cannot work against it if we have put it in place. A vow is a vow, for good or for evil. **We must break ungodly vows and repent that we made an inner vow that put us over that area as King.** And we must allow God the opportunity to rule in that area and trust Him with it. Then we will receive the blessings and the freedom God intended for us. Only when we break that inner vow and release our wounded souls over to God will we be healed and set free.

There's good news. If you have bitterness in your heart because you were wounded and made an inner vow, if you want it broken, the love and forgiveness God provides for you will break that inner vow.

Let's work through it…

▷ *Are there any inner vows keeping you from experiencing breakthrough or the love of God in a specific area? Write out any that come to mind, and ask Holy Spirit to examine them with you.*

▷ *Are you willing to dethrone yourself from areas of woundedness, allow God to rule over them and to bring you healing and deliverance?*

▷ *Take the time to repent for playing God in that area of your life and ask God to take His rightful place to be King over the throne of your heart.*

HOW DO YOU THINK YOUR LIFE COULD CHANGE WHEN YOU LET GOD BE KING OVER THOSE AREAS?

Know Your Enemy, Walk in Authority

Goals:

- ▸ Stop the game and stop hiding from God
- ▸ Break your agreement with generational curses
- ▸ Be on guard and protect what's yours
- ▸ Live from the inside out

DON'T PITCH A TENT THERE

12

THE GOAL: STOP THE GAME AND STOP HIDING FROM GOD

———

"Adam, where are you?"

Read Genesis chapters 1:26–3:24.

Some of you know the story well; others maybe have never read it. Let me give you some of the highlights or refresh your memory…

We meet Adam and his beautiful wife, Eve. God created them, and He called them "really good." Nothing in all of His creation came close to His spectacular masterpiece of humanity.

They walked and talked with Him daily. He gave them charge over all the animals and gardens. Adam and Eve were God's creation, and they were free to enjoy all of God's goodness in the garden. And what a garden that must have been! What a calling and a purpose for the first human beings of the world!

Adam and Eve had the honor and privilege of being in the presence of the Almighty God, of walking in His divine love, of experiencing peace and joy every single day. Life was good. Life was *perfect* in every sense of that word. Perfect.

Well, someone—he's called "the serpent" here in Genesis and is known as the devil, the deceiver, a liar, the enemy of God—was not too happy about the perfect love relationship Adam and Eve had with God. He decided to try to destroy it. He schemed to tempt them to betray God with beautiful, delicious-looking fruit from one of God's very own trees in the middle of the garden.

What?! Adam and Eve were tempted by *fruit?*

Well, yes and no…

The deceiver, Satan, promised them if they ate the fruit, they would be like God.

Uh, were they not already filled with God's spirit? His love, goodness, authority and all that they needed to be and to live?

Yes, they were! So can you see the deceit and the lies from Satan which blinded them to the truth?

It wasn't so much the delicious fruit that tempted Adam and Eve: it was *the lie* behind the whole scene that tempted them. Satan used what was a truth (that they were already created in His image; had dominion over all He created…), turned it into a lie, and thereby turned them against God. What's so mind-blowing in this is that they bought the lie!

Satan is good at that. **He takes a little bit of what we know to be truth and twists it into a lie so that it still sounds like truth, but it isn't!** Because he does that, it is vital that we *know* what the Word of God says and not just guess what it says. It's not enough to go to church to hear a message preached, or to tune into a favorite preacher on YouTube or on the radio or on a podcast. We need to know the Word of God for ourselves, so when the enemy tries to twist God's truth, we would know it immediately and not fall for his lies! We also need the gift of discernment, which is the ability to recognize what is good, what is evil, what is truth and what is a lie.

Adam and Eve bought into the lie. They obviously thought that being made in God's image and having all dominion over all God gave them wasn't enough, so they gave in to the temptation and the lie. When they did, they broke the perfect unity and relationship they had with God. What a moment in time—it was a moment that affected all of humanity's earthly and eternal condition!

Listening in just for a moment and giving in to Satan's lies against you can change the whole course of your life, and not for the better...

Adam and Eve realized all of that, I'm sure. But it was too late. Their perfect relationship, their perfect union was broken, and they could not bear the guilt of it.

So what did they do? They hid. Because they felt so ashamed and condemned, they didn't even want to be with God. I believe they thought He would be angry and reject them. I believe, knowing they betrayed Him, their hearts hurt. They'd never experienced hurt with Him before. How could they have done that to Him? To themselves? So, they covered themselves with fig leaves and hid.

Fig leaves... they tried to cover their sin with a physical covering—hoping God wouldn't see it. We do the same. We try to cover our sin with physical stuff (good works, the right words, religious prayers, etc.) so that maybe the sin wouldn't be so obvious or maybe God would overlook it. But it doesn't work that way, does it?

Brokenness makes us feel shame and want to hide... This still happens between God and us today.

Well, God saw what happened, and He came looking for and calling out to Adam.

"Where are you?" (Genesis 3:9 ESV)

Please note that this is a key question: "Where are you?"

It's not like God, who is omniscient, didn't know where Adam was, but I believe He wanted Adam to come forward and be honest. **You can't be honest when you're hiding.**

I once heard a preacher say that God came out walking to the same place He and Adam had been meeting at every day, expecting Adam to still show up—no matter what had happened. I personally believe God desired Adam to have unbroken fellowship with Him even when Adam failed Him. It's not like God didn't know, but I wonder if the very act of God walking into the garden, showing up like He always did at that time and calling out for Adam, wasn't to show Adam that God still loved him and desired a relationship with him. I wonder...

When God asks the question, "Where are you?" He desires more than anything for us to be there, to meet Him and say, "I'm here, God. I messed up, but I'm still here. I'm so sorry. I need your help..." And He wants us to keep walking with Him.

Maybe it's time to come out of hiding and answer His question, honestly...

"My son, my daughter, where are you? I'm looking for you."

I'm here, God, just where I've always been. Just where we've been meeting from the time You created me. I'm here, in Your presence. I don't want to run away and hide. I'm right here. But I need You more than ever.

They played the blame game

When Adam and Eve came out of hiding, I believe they should have had *that* conversation with God. But in Genesis 3, we see it was a very different conversation. It was a blame-shift type of conversation filled with guilt, shame and regret. But it didn't have to be that way. We know now (because the Bible tells us) to confess our sins so that we will be healed. Adam and Eve chose to hide and blame-shift instead. (Pride and fear will do that to you.) It didn't accomplish any healing or redemption for them. Instead, they had to go through difficult and unpleasant consequences. We still experience those consequences today.

Adam blamed Eve for what happened. Eve blamed the Serpent for what happened, and no one took responsibility for what they each did. No one wanted to "own it" and receive the forgiveness and the restoration they needed from God.

Sin messes with God's pure, heavenly plans for us. That's Satan's plan for us: to destroy our relationship with God so that we will live outside of His divine will for our lives. Jesus said this:

> The thief comes only to steal and kill and destroy; I have come that they may have life, and have it to the full. (John 10:10 NIV)

If fear captures you, it can lead you away from Him

After their conversation with God, Adam and Eve weren't allowed to live in Eden anymore. They were to live outside of the perfect garden God had created for them to live in for eternity. They had to move outside the garden and begin living in a physical manner where they would experience physical labor, pain and ultimately physical death.

God never wanted those consequences, but He is a just God and He gave mankind free will to choose Him. Adam and Eve chose the lies of the enemy. What a hot mess they got themselves into—not to mention the rest of mankind, too! **Sin costs us dearly, and unless we place ourselves under the perfect love and blood of Jesus, sin will continue to rule and mess up our lives for generations to come.**

This is a thought that has forever changed my relationship with God: The unconditional love of God seen here is unfathomable! As God was creating Adam, He knew that this being He was creating was going to betray Him. In fact, He knew that from Adam on, all of the world would have a choice to choose Him and to be with Him forever or to reject Him and live separate from Him for eternity. While God was creating Adam with His very own heart and hands, He was taking the risk of being betrayed and rejected by His very own creation, yet He continued with His plan. Oh, how great is the love of the Father toward us!

Let's work through it...

God's love is not like man's love. It's not conditional. It doesn't love only when you're good, or good enough, or almost perfect. He loves you in spite of any failure of yours, and He loves you with His everlasting love.

> ▷ *God is asking you, "Where are you?" His desire is for you to come out of hiding, be with Him and have an honest, open relationship with Him. Take some time and consider areas you might be hiding from God, or lies from Satan you might have believed. Confess them here.*
>
> ▷ *Do you find yourself playing the blame game? How can you stop that?*
>
> ▷ *What are some lies the devil has told you that you've been believing? How can you stop living from those lies?*

Only the truth of what God's Word says to you and about you will counteract and defeat the enemy's lies against you.

> ▷ *What are some scriptures that speak of God's unconditional love for you? Write them down and take some time to meditate on them.*

HOW CAN YOU GROW DEEPER IN THE LOVING RELATIONSHIP GOD DESIRES TO HAVE WITH YOU?

13

THE GOAL: BREAK YOUR AGREEMENT WITH GENERATIONAL CURSES

———

I heard about generational curses. Are they real? Do they have power over me? Can I turn this around in my life or am I doomed to this end, too?

Many people struggle with the question, "Is there such a thing as generational curses?"

Generational curses are the work of demonic spirits which have been allowed to operate through multiple generations. Within the same family, they repeat their influence through *open doors* which the enemy works through. Examples include alcoholism, abusive behavior, addictions, lust, greed, anger, unforgiveness, manipulation, etc. These are all works of the devil. They sure aren't from God! But you may be thinking, "Well, these aren't really generational curses. They are choices we make on our own. Why should we involve the devil in this?"

I agree that these are sometimes choices we make of our own will. But take a close look at *what* we choose, then: the things that bring us harm, torment, judgment etc… those things are rooted in evil, not good, which means these behaviors or strongholds are rooted in the demonic realm. Let's not kid around with this. When we choose opposite of what is godly, we choose what is of the evil one. Yes, we choose. But just like Adam and Eve *chose* to give in to the temptation to rebel against God, the devil was behind it all. That temptation to sin was planned by the devil himself. Don't be fooled that it's just your choice or my choice or "the flesh." **Anything that can cause destruction and harm to us and keep us from the life God designed for us is rooted in evil.** When you begin to realize that the same evil addiction had been and is presently working through your great-grandfather, your grandfather, your father and your uncles to destroy them (the same exact "issue" manifested throughout the generations and the years), it's more than just a poor choice that they have *all* made or are making. Sometimes it's an evil spirit assigned to the family to ultimately destroy it. (a generational curse). I have personally witnessed the manifestation of it in several families I have ministered to over the years. This demonic spirit or curse must be dealt with through the only thing that can eradicate it from you forever—the blood of Jesus, the finished work of the cross. **The enemy uses these things to destroy the body, soul and spirit, and we can't bury our heads in the sand and pretend it's not a real thing.**

But there's good news! First John 3:8 says: "But the Son of God came to destroy the works of the devil" (NLT).

Jesus came to destroy the works of the devil

So, although generational curses are a real thing, I don't believe they have any power over your life *if* you believe in Jesus, have been reborn of His spirit and have by the power and blood of Jesus broken that curse off of you forever. Some of your family members, past and present, may have chosen to live with these curses, but you don't have to. You've been set free by the power of Jesus and the finished work of the cross!

But it seems that what's been over my family is over me, too! I'm a believer in Jesus, so what's up with this?

One reason you might experience what looks like or what may feel like a generational curse in your life is that you may be *agreeing* with it by *choosing* to live under it. Let me explain further.

The power of agreement

If you agree with the work of the enemy (a generational curse) that is working through your family and now seems to be over you, it may be that you are keeping that same door open for him to work it in your own life as well.

What does agreeing with the enemy look like in this situation? Every time something negative or evil happens to you or to your family members, you acknowledge or affirm it by saying and believing it has power. *"See? I knew this family is cursed! Now I have to deal with this too!"* Or, *"Well, my dad told me to expect it because it's just my lot in life."* Or, *"It's bound to happen to me if it happened to my mother or my grandfather. It's just the way it is. It's our fate in this family. I can't escape it. My dad's an alcoholic and that's why I'm one too! Can't help it! It's played out throughout our generations. My mom struggled with that disease all her life, and so did aunty Jane. It's just in our family's genes. It can't be helped. If my mom and my aunts died in their 50s, so will I."* Etc. etc.

Do you see how that type of thinking and speaking (words *create*, remember?) is agreeing with the work of the enemy? By giving in to the demonic work, by giving in to a generational curse that's been allowed to accomplish its assignment in your family, by giving it a voice, you give it permission and you give it the power to keep working. That is agreeing with it.

Are you in unity with God or with the devil?

Remember, your words create life or death. The Bible tells us this. (We talk more about that in the session on the Power of Your Words). *Agreement is a powerful thing!* Unity is God's principle. **When we come into agreement with something or someone, we come into unity with it.** That's why we are warned in 2 Corinthians 6:14–16(a) not to unite or come into agreement with people or things that are not of God. Take a look:

Don't continue to team up with unbelievers in mismatched alliances, for what partnership is there between righteousness and rebellion? Who could mingle light with darkness? What harmony can there be between Christ and Satan? Or what does a believer have in common with an unbeliever? What friendship does God's temple have with demons? (TPT)

This is how powerful unity and agreement are. **God established it so that we would come into agreement with Him and His Word alone, that it might bring us life.** But the enemy will try everything he can to keep us separated from God. So he will try to live in a family line as long as he's given the permission to do so. The enemy knows how agreement works. He knows it is powerful enough to create or establish a stronghold, so he abuses it to achieve his own evil plans against us. Let's be wise against this!

In order to break agreement with the enemy, you must believe in Jesus, live in Him, and obey Him. "If you love Me, obey my commandments," Jesus says (John 14:15 NLT).

You must not entangle yourself with demonic things that cause harm, death or destruction. In order to break agreement with the enemy, you must separate yourself from him and break the authority your family or you have given to him over the years.

Jesus canceled out every demonic work against you on the cross!

You must come into agreement with what Jesus did for you. You must come into agreement with what Jesus says in His Word about removing all sin and curses against you. We must deal with the generational curse by receiving, believing and applying the truth found in Colossians 2:12–15 (TPT; emphasis mine):

For we've been buried with him into his death. Our "baptism into death" also means we were raised with him when we believed in God's resurrection power, the power that raised him from death's realm. This "realm of death" describes our former state, for we were held in sin's grasp. But now, we've been resurrected out of that "realm of death" never to return, for we are forever alive and forgiven of all our sins!

He canceled out every legal violation we had on our record and the old arrest warrant that stood to indict us. He erased it all—our sins, our stained soul—he deleted it all, and they cannot be retrieved! Everything we once were in Adam has been placed onto his cross and nailed permanently there as a public display of cancellation.

Then Jesus made a public spectacle of all the powers and principalities of darkness, stripping away from them every weapon and all their spiritual authority and power to accuse us. And by the power of the cross, Jesus led them around as prisoners in a procession of triumph. He was not their prisoner; they were his!

The key to live free from any generational curse is to come into agreement with the Word of God; to agree with what Jesus did on the cross for you; "canceling out every legal violation we had on our record and the old arrest warrant that stood to indict us. He erased it all—our sins, our stained soul—he deleted it all and they cannot be retrieved! Everything we once were in Adam has been placed onto his cross and nailed permanently there as a public display of cancellation" (Col. 2:14 TPT).

If you continue to agree with the work of the enemy that he's been allowed to do throughout your family, then he has *legal* access to continue, not because he's more powerful than Jesus, but because *you* are allowing him by not believing that Jesus triumphed over the enemy and from that truth, canceling out his legal right to you.

The spirit of unbelief

How else do you agree with the enemy? If you have a spirit of unbelief towards who Jesus is and all He is or can be to you, then you are agreeing with the devil. If you don't believe and activate what we just read about what Jesus did to defeat the enemy, then the enemy has legal right to continue to harass you through the generational curse. The Word says in Matthew 12:30 that if you are not for God, you are against Him. **When the spirit of unbelief is in you, then how can you defeat the enemy with truth if the truth of Jesus is not found in you?**

> You do not have His word abiding in you, for you do not believe Him whom He sent. (John 5:38 NASB)

> And without faith it is impossible to please Him, for he who comes to God must believe that He is and that He is a rewarder of those who seek Him. (Hebrews 11:6 NASB)

> But though He had performed so many signs before them, yet they were not believing in Him. (John 12:37 NASB)

> So we see that they were not able to enter because of unbelief. (Hebrews 3:19 NASB)

Unless you believe, apply and walk in all that Jesus did for you, the enemy will continue to lie to you and harass you—until *you* put a stop to it! And Jesus made a way so you can. It's called believing and walking in the truth, and it will set you free.

Take your authority in Jesus

If you are in a personal relationship with Jesus Christ and you live your life based on the absolute truth of who He is and have received all He's done for you, you are authorized and empowered by Him to stop demonic spirits from continuing to rule and reign in your life regardless of the evil you have seen or experienced in your family's life.

Jesus paid a hefty price to take back the authority which Adam and Eve gave up to Satan when they gave in to sin. Jesus gives that spiritual authority back to you, His child, when you receive Him into your life as your personal Savior and Lord.

Not all believers understand what having this authority means. Without an understanding and a sincere belief in *the power of the cross*, they may continue to believe the lies of the enemy and stay under the influence of generational curses. The enemy will retain his stronghold over them. They will continue to rationalize the problem by saying something like: "It's just in the family," or "My dad and my grandfather dealt with it. I guess I have to live with it too."

I have seen too many people submit to those lies because that's the way their family does things or operates, which causes them to live under burdens of mental, emotional, physical and spiritual defeat for all their lives. The enemy is a liar, and we need to recognize his lies in our own lives and stop giving him the power to!

Put an end to the assignment of the enemy in your life

I've also seen people come into agreement with what Jesus did for them, take their authority in Him, cast those evil spirits out and put an end to the evil assignments of destruction against them and their family.

If we live and operate from the authority that Jesus has given to us, a familiar spirit or generational curse which has been permitted to wreak havoc through our family can no longer operate.

The enemy must surrender and flee in the name and authority of Jesus Christ when that authority is *activated* by the believer.

If I am fully surrendered to God (and that is key!), and I live for Him and with Him, then I have His power within me to resist the enemy, and he must flee from me!

> Submit yourselves, then, to God. Resist the devil, and he will flee from you. (James 4:7 NIV)

> Now you understand that I have imparted to you all my authority to trample over his kingdom. You will trample upon every demon before you and overcome every power Satan possesses. Absolutely

nothing will be able to harm you as you walk in this authority. (Luke 10:19 TPT)

As I mentioned at the beginning of this chapter, I'm not saying that all problems are directly thrust on us "from the devil." Some are definitely the workings of our own foolish choices, which are rooted in evil. And if we are true followers of Jesus, we would know the difference.

We bring problems on ourselves sometimes through our own rebellion, selfish choices and foolishness. If not dealt with, the consequences of these choices and behaviors can destroy our lives. For all of these problems, we need to apply the wisdom and authority of God so we can overcome them. But in this session, we are trying to answer the question, "Is there such a thing as generational curses?"

There definitely are generational curses that run rampant throughout families, but those are only in effect for those who continue to agree with the enemy and allow him to continue on. It is important to note that because we are children of God doesn't mean the enemy just goes away and doesn't bother with us anymore. Far from it! It's a real thing. It's rooted in the spiritual realm. We were created spiritual beings. We can't bury our heads in the sand and live in fantasy land, thinking we are free from the effects of evil in our lifetime. **We shouldn't put focus on the devil, but we need to be aware of his schemes against us and know that we've been given victory through Jesus Christ over him.**

The Bible explains it this way:

> For our struggle is not against flesh and blood, but against the rulers, against the authorities, against the powers of this dark world and against the spiritual forces of evil in the heavenly realms. (Ephesians 6:12 NIV)

So how do we break free from these generational curses in our lives?

- By believing that Jesus already made us free from them at the cross
- By breaking our agreement with them through the power of Jesus
- By taking and living in the authority that Jesus gave us over them

Let's work through it...

> ▷ What can help you determine if an issue in your life is a result of an act of your own rebellion or foolishness, or if it's an issue that you are in agreement with the influence of the demonic, as we know it to be a "generational curse"?
> ▷ Are you in agreement with all that Jesus did on the cross for you?

HOW ARE YOU EXERCISING THE AUTHORITY JESUS GAVE TO YOU, OR HOW CAN YOU BEGIN TO APPLY IT?

14

THE GOAL: BE ON GUARD AND PROTECT WHAT IS YOURS

There is a Bible verse that warns us about the thief coming to steal, kill and destroy. You may have heard it or read about it. Have you ever wondered who the thief is? We have an enemy. He is an enemy of God and his name is Satan or the devil. Many would laugh and scoff at this, saying he's not real. Let's take a moment to look and observe the world around us. The evil found in it is not of God. The depth of this evil cannot even be conjured up from the heart of the vilest man. No. It comes from our enemy, the devil and he is very real. It would be a good thing for each of us to understand this. This session is not to glorify him in any way, but to help you be aware of how you can win against him when he tries to steal from and destroy your life. God is so much greater than he is! That's why it's so important to know how God has provided for us to be equipped to stand against our enemy and win!

You were not created only as a human, but you were also created a spiritual being. That means that as you grow in Christ, a spiritual battle goes on around you every day. Sometimes, that battle is over you. Jesus gave us a lot of instruction and direction on how to fight the enemy. It's not something to ignore or to be fearful of. It's important to know what may be causing you to feel depressed or angry or stuck and not able to move forward. So, let's examine the biblical truths to help us move forward in our lives. Let's discover some of the spiritual weapons God provides to overcome the enemy's schemes against you.

Part one of John 10:10 reads: "The thief comes to steal, kill and destroy."

The enemy has a strategy. He had one at the beginning when he tried to get between Adam and Eve and God. He applied it then, and it worked. He does the same thing today. We need to recognize his tricks and not be defeated!

He comes to steal

He is called a *thief*. What is he out to steal? Well, many things, but today I want to discuss one of them. **If the devil can steal from you the truth of who God is and who you are in God, he begins to access territory in your life.** That territory is your mind.

That's where he usually starts. He plants lies into your mind.

Here's what scripture says:

> But now I'm afraid that just as Eve was deceived by the serpent's clever lies, your thoughts may be corrupted, and you may lose your single-hearted devotion and pure love for Christ. (2 Corinthians 11:3 TPT)

> … He's been a murderer right from the start! He never stood with the One who is the true Prince, for he's full of nothing but lies—lying is his native tongue. He is a master of deception and the father of lies! (John 8:44 TPT)

Your enemy the devil is a liar. With the help of Holy Spirit, you can discern his lies. That's why it's so important for you to have a personal, intimate relationship with Jesus- then His Spirit can protect you from the schemes of the enemy. But you need to *know* and *believe* the Word of God for your life so that through it, you can stop the enemy from stealing from you!

A thief is only considered to be stealing when he takes something that is not rightfully his. If it's rightfully his, he wouldn't be stealing, would he?

So, does your mind belong to the devil or to Jesus? Meaning - who owns your thoughts? Your belief system? Who are you giving power over your mind? I'm hoping you have the mind of Christ and that you would OWN the truth of His Word in your life. If you OWN the truth of who God says He is and who you are in Him, then the enemy cannot steal it from you! He will try and try and try, but unless you *willingly* give up ownership of the truth, he cannot take it from you!

> Stand firm then, with the **belt of truth** buckled around your waist...
> (Ephesians 6:14 NLT)

> In every battle, take faith as your wrap-around shield, for it is able to extinguish the blazing arrows coming at you from the Evil One!
> (Ephesians 6:16 TPT)

If the enemy can convince you to get you to the point of unbelief about who God says He is and all He says in His word, if he can get you to give up on that truth, then he has succeeded in his first step—stealing from you the very foundation of your life.

He can then move on to the second part of his game plan against you.

It's so important for you to discover through the Word, and through your daily relationship with Him, who God is: who He says He is, what He looks like, what He's done, and what He's doing in your life. When you know God through a personal relationship, you will believe Him and learn to trust Him. When you trust Him to be absolute truth in your life, nothing and no demon in hell can shake that truth from you or deceive you.

> This is good, and pleases God our Savior, who wants all people to be saved and to come to a knowledge of the truth. (1 Timothy 2:3–4 NIV)

Jesus answered, "I am the way and the truth and the life. No one comes to the Father except through me." (John 14:6 NIV)

...You will know the truth, and the truth will set you free. (John 8:32 NIV)

He comes to kill

Here is a warning scripture we must pay attention to:

Before you were led astray, you were so faithful to Messiah. Why have you now turned away from what is right and true? Who has deceived you? (Galatians 5:7 TPT)

More lies from the enemy! If he can steal the truth from you of who God is and who you are in God, then he will work to kill any plans that God has for you.

Because think about it: If you believe there is no God or that God doesn't really care about you, that His Word and His promises are not real, then what's the point in believing that He has plans for your life? **It's the enemy's plans to try to kill any dream or plan that God has for you.** He doesn't want you living out the plans of God for your life. The devil doesn't want you to fulfill God's purposes for your life or living a life that honors God.

Guard the plans God has for you!

You need to know from God's Word what God says about His plans for your life! You need to believe that you don't just exist, but that God wants you to thrive in all He's called you to! Remember Psalm 139 and Jeremiah 29:11 from the beginning of this section? God wrote, knows and planned every day of your life for your good, for a hope and a purpose!

Now may the God of peace, who through the blood of the eternal covenant brought back from the dead our Lord Jesus, that great

Shepherd of the sheep, equip you with every good thing to do His will. And may He accomplish in us what is pleasing in His sight through Jesus Christ, to whom be glory forever and ever. Amen. (Hebrews 13:20–21 NIV)

For we are God's handiwork, created in Christ Jesus to do good works, which God prepared in advance for us to do. (Ephesians 2:10 NIV)

He comes to destroy

The word *destroy* means "to ruin the structure, organic existence, or condition of" and "to put out of existence" (see Merriam-Webster.com).

This is what the enemy's plans for you are: to put you out of existence and to ruin your life or the condition of it. He hates that you love God and want Him in your life. He hates that you believe that God created you in His image and wants to stop you from reflecting Him. He is a liar and a deceiver. Think of it this way: BEWARE OF DOG!

Do you see what that means in (your) real life? There is a dog out there, and if you get on his property, he will attack you. You can't risk not believing he's real or whether he's out there or not. Jesus said the devil is real, so you need to guard yourself. How can you do this?

Be intentional to get up from any discouragement and spirit of defeat that's beat you down and stand up for what is God's truth in your life!

Live by His truth and by the Spirit of God within you! Counteract the enemy's lies with the truth and learn to live from the Word of God. Why do I keep using and repeating the word 'truth'? It's because the devil is a liar (Jesus even called him 'the father of lies'). So if the devil is a liar, then everything he throws at you is a lie so the only way to win and overcome him is by operating from the truth of God! TRUTH WINS!

Guard the truth of God's Word with your life. Own it. Own who God is in your life. Own the truth of who you are in Christ. Guard the promises of God for your future. Guard your life so that the thief cannot come in and steal it from you!

Let's work through it...

Consider the following scriptures:

> Be alert and of sober mind. Your enemy the devil prowls around like a roaring lion looking for someone to devour. (1 Peter 5:8 NIV)

> For our struggle is not against flesh and blood, but against the rulers, against the authorities, against the powers of this dark world and against the spiritual forces of evil in the heavenly realms. (Ephesians 6:12 NIV)

> ▷ *What do you think the enemy stealing from you looks like?*
> ▷ *Have you allowed the enemy to steal from you? If so, how?*
> ▷ *How are you guarding yourself against this "dog," your enemy?*

HOW ARE YOU OWNING THE TRUTH AND THE RELATIONSHIP YOU HAVE WITH JESUS?

15

THE GOAL: LIVE FROM THE INSIDE OUT

———

The following is both a practical and spiritual exercise I use with clients when I coach them to help them understand how the body, soul and spirit are intricately linked. When any one part is not healthy, the other parts suffer as well.

Take a look at the diagram. Refer to it as you read through the following to understand the significance of it in relation to your own life.

John 10:10 THE THIEF COMES ONLY TO STEAL AND KILL AND DESTROY; I HAVE COME THAT THEY MAY HAVE LIFE, AND HAVE IT TO THE FULL.

The enemy works from the Outside In

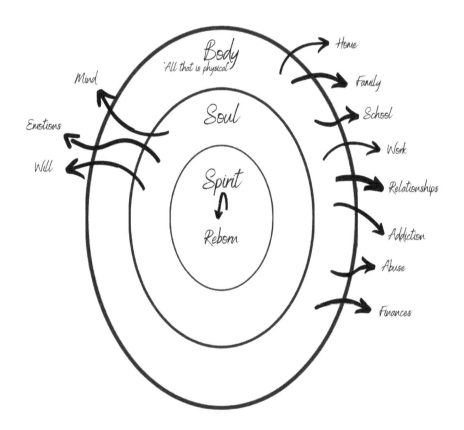

Jesus works from the Inside Out

I base this illustration of body, soul and spirit on John 10:10 (NIV): "The thief comes only to steal and kill and destroy; I have come that they may have life, and have it to the full."

As shown on the diagram, I believe the enemy works to destroy from the outside in, but Jesus works to bring healing and restoration from the inside out.

Body, soul, and spirit

You are made up of three parts:

- Your body – All that is physical in your life or has physically happened to you
- Your soul – Your mind/thoughts, emotions and will
- Your spirit – As a believer in Jesus, the part of you that is reborn of His Spirit.

Let's break each of these down.

#1 – BODY: The physical part of you (refer to the diagram)

To address the body, we must address the whole of physical life. By *physical life*, I mean to include all bodily, substantive, material, and environmental things that you experience and live in or with, that have the potential to affect your body.

To get a grasp of the concept, think about what has been or still may be negative in your physical life. For example, you might think of negative experiences that have physically happened and affected you, such as abusive or irrational behaviors and choices inflicted on you by your parents, teachers, brothers, sisters or anyone else who contributed to your life in some negative way. Perhaps you'll think of where you live(d), if you've moved all over the country and never had a stable address, or if you've lived in physical chaos, in poverty or in a militant, or in an unreasonable perfectionist environment. You may have experienced or are experiencing personal addictions, lack of finances, physical abuse, toxic or unhealthy relationships, homelessness, poor self-image, betrayal in friendships, bullying at school, the pressure to compromise personal values in the workplace. You might think of anything that has made and still makes up your *physical, bodily* life that has had a traumatic or a negative effect.

If you find you have issues in this area, I encourage you to face them with godly counsel. If you don't deal with physical-level issues that cause you direct harm, to feel wounded, to feel depression, abandonment, hate, etc., those issues will impact and influence your soul (your mind, emotions, and will) and can become a root cause of absolute defeat and loss in your life. Godly counsel and understanding what I'm explaining here can help jump start your way to healing and freedom.

How can what happened to you in the physical realm affect your soul? Let's look at that next.

#2 – SOUL: Your mind, emotions and will (refer to the diagram)

When something happens to us *physically*, we usually attach an emotion to that event. If our thoughts about a physically-based event are toxic, and we don't deal with them, then our emotions will agree with our thoughts.

When they do, we will *feel* depressed, unloved, unappreciated, sorry for ourselves, hurt, angry, frustrated… In turn, those emotions will affect our will.

If our thoughts are negative, and our emotions are in agreement with that negativity, we will give in and we will operate from negativity. That's how our will then gets involved.

Thoughts – emotions – will - For example:

If our thoughts are filled with hate, and our emotions are in agreement with those thoughts of hatred, we more than likely will give in to them and operate from a spirit of hatred.

We will have no desire—no will—to forgive, to do good, to be kind, to have compassion, to overcome or to make the right choices. We will surrender to the destructive thoughts of hate.

When your soul is in agreement with all that's happened to you physically, and you are not surrendered to Holy Spirit, a foothold for the enemy forms. This is what I mean when I say that the enemy works from the outside – in. **It's not so much that he himself does all the dirty work directly to harm you, but he *uses* all the negatives that are in your life to destroy you if you refuse to move from that state** (that's the kind of foothold he looks for). He will use, for instance, a broken relationship, abuse, addiction, lack of finances, the absence of your father, feelings of abandonment, that guy who bullied you at school or any other negative physical thing that's happened to lie to you and keep you stuck so that you feel you're not able to move forward from any of it.

So how do you move forward from your negative "outside" life towards healing and freedom?

The change starts in your soul, namely your mind, for where your mind goes, all else follows. Do you know how powerful your mind is?

What you *think* about your life determines what kind of life you live.

Dr. Caroline Leaf is a cognitive neuroscientist with a Ph.D. in Communication Pathology specializing in Neuropsychology who has helped thousands, if not millions, change their lives by helping them change their minds, one thought at a time.

Here are a few of her quotes that, when practiced, have the ability to change a person's life just by changing their thoughts.

> *We are not victims of our biology. We are co-creators of our destiny alongside God. God leads, but we have to choose to let God lead. We have been designed to create thoughts, and from these we live out our lives (Prov. 23:7).*

Reaction is the key word here. You cannot control the events or circumstances of your life, but you can control your reactions.

Your body is not in control of your mind—your mind is in control of your body, and your mind is stronger than your body. Mind certainly is over matter.[2]

How you *think* about all that's happened in your life will determine the course of your life. If you think you'll never get over it, never heal from it, never be able to forgive or forget, then that's exactly how you'll live. Not because you can't live in freedom, but because you refuse to—because (you may *think*) it's easier to fall victim to your circumstance than to fight for freedom from it.

If you think that it's too much, too late or too unresolvable, then the enemy will continue to use these things and literally destroy you – from the outside in! Is that what you want? Is that what God has called you to?

Change your thoughts, change your life

We've all heard that expression, *Change your thoughts, change your life.* It's a difficult thing to do, but it is truth. If you submit your mind to the mind of Christ, your emotions and your will follow. What does that mean exactly? When we became born again, we became new creatures. The old has gone, the new has come.

For, "Who has known the mind of the Lord so as to instruct him?" But we have the mind of Christ. (1 Corinthians 2:16 NIV)

Therefore, if anyone is in Christ, the new creation has come: The old has gone, the new is here! (2 Corinthians 5:17 NIV)

We then received the Holy Spirit, the mind of Christ, to be able to live according to His spirit, not having to live in the flesh anymore, not having to live in darkness anymore. When you take on the mind of

---

[2] Caroline Leaf, *Switch on Your Brain: The Key to Peak Happiness, Thinking, and Health* (Grand Rapids, MI: Baker Publishing Group, 2015).

Christ, you will find yourself happier, freer, more at peace, less stressed, more loving and a whole lot more positive than you ever thought you could be. Your circumstances don't define you as long as you believe that and live according to the Spirit of God within you.

Total transformation

The Word of God renews your mind. If you allow it to, it washes it clean, making it pure until you are thinking godly, healthy and excellent thoughts—thoughts that bring healing to your soul.

> And now, dear brothers and sisters, one final thing. Fix your thoughts on what is true, and honorable, and right, and pure, and lovely, and admirable. Think about things that are excellent and worthy of praise. Keep putting into practice all you learned and received from me—everything you heard from me and saw me doing. Then the God of peace will be with you. (Philippians 4:8–9 NLT)

When you start to renew your mind, you will experience the peace of God—no matter what you went through or are going through. This is a promise we can find in Philippians 4:4–9.

When you are TRANSFORMED by the power of Holy Spirit from the inside, then you have access to think with the mind of Jesus and gain victory over all that's trying to defeat you that's from the "outside"; the physical.

When you are transformed by the power of Holy Spirit, you have the authority to cancel out every lie from the enemy against you.

As your mind becomes renewed and filled with light, you will be able to think differently. Scripture says, "Your eye is like a lamp that provides light for your body. When your eye is healthy, your whole body is filled with light" (Matthew 6:22 NLT).

You will have a new perspective of all the physical that's happened (or is happening) to you, and with the Word and power of Holy Spirit, you will be able to OVERCOME all the negative the enemy has devised against you.

Being a DOER of the Word is KEY

The Word of God is full of wisdom, light and guidance to help us navigate through all parts of life with success. So, let's start with submitting our minds and bodies to God, for He alone knows us better than we know ourselves.

In Romans 12:1–2, the apostle Paul encourages the church:

> Beloved friends, what should be our proper response to God's marvelous mercies? To surrender yourselves to God to be his sacred, living sacrifices. And live in holiness, experiencing all that delights his heart. For this becomes your genuine expression of worship. Stop imitating the ideals and opinions of the culture around you, but be inwardly transformed by the Holy Spirit through a total reformation of how you think. This will empower you to discern God's will as you live a beautiful life, satisfying and perfect in his eyes. (TPT)

In Corinthians, he says this:

> We demolish arguments and every pretension that sets itself up against the knowledge of God, and we take captive every thought to make it obedient to Christ. (2 Corinthians 10:5 NIV)

It's important that we participate with the Holy Spirit in our lives to move towards victory and freedom.

> But be doers of the word, and not hearers only, deceiving yourselves. For if anyone is a hearer of the word and not a doer, he is like a man observing his natural face in a mirror; for he observes himself, goes away, and immediately forgets what kind of man he was. But he who looks into the perfect law of liberty and continues in it, and is not a forgetful hearer but a doer of the work, this one will be blessed in what he does. (James 1:22–25 NKJV)

If you live and operate your life from the outside,(the physical), focusing on what's happened to you, you don't get closer to being the whole person God designed you to be. The negative things that you have gone through, although painful, can be used as learning experiences, stepping stones or building blocks that, in God's hands, could lead you to a better life: the life God designed for you. Allowing the Word of God to change your mind about your life will bring about the healing and joy you've been praying for. This doesn't mean you live in denial of what you've gone through, but it means that the enemy doesn't get to use it against you anymore.

#3 – SPIRIT: *The part of you which is REBORN of the Spirit of God (refer to the diagram)*

When you receive Jesus Christ as your Lord and Savior, you are *reborn* of His Spirit; the enemy cannot touch your spirit. You are sealed with Holy Spirit. If you are reborn and you die today, you will be with Jesus for the rest of eternity. But there's more to it. You are to grow in your relationship with Jesus so that you become the reflection of His image from the inside out. You grow to look like and live like Him every day. In order for that to happen, your spirit man on the inside begins to take over your soul. **The Spirit of God within you who is helping you get stronger in Him and more like Him gets to call the shots on what's going on with you—if you allow Him to.** If you begin to think or feel or behave negatively, then your spirit man pulls up God's Word (all that is pure, true, trustworthy, honest....) and has the power to overtake your destructive thoughts, emotions and will. But you must take that authority and allow Holy Spirit to flow through and within you.

Jesus works from the INSIDE OUT! (refer to the diagram)

When you are *reborn* of His spirit, you become a new creation. The old, the past, is gone.

Jesus works from the inside out. You are sealed with Holy Spirit. This is a hope and a promise for those who are in Jesus. The Spirit of God can begin to work from the inside out, overtaking all that's been evil or negative in your life to set you free and make all things work together for your good.

These are His promises to you as a new creation in Christ!

> Now, if anyone is enfolded into Christ, he has become an entirely new creation. All that is related to the old order has vanished. Behold, everything is fresh and new. (2 Corinthians 5:17 TPT)

> I am doing something brand new, something unheard of. Even now it sprouts and grows and matures. Don't you perceive it? (Isaiah 43:19 TPT)

> And in Him, having heard and believed the word of truth— the gospel of your salvation— you were sealed with the promised Holy Spirit, who is the pledge of our inheritance until the redemption of those who are God's possession, to the praise of His glory. (Ephesians 1:12–13 NIV)

> And He who searches our hearts knows the mind of the Spirit, because the Spirit intercedes for the saints according to the will of God. And we know that God works all things together for the good of those who love Him, who are called according to His purpose. (Romans 8:27–28 NIV)

So let's put it all together and watch how this works!

Your SPIRIT, which is reborn of God, now begins to influence and empower your SOUL and gives courage to your WILL.

As you read, meditate and apply the Word of God, it will replace all the bitter, hateful, angry thoughts about what happened to you in the PHYSICAL realm. In essence, you are becoming "new" as Jesus said you would.

Those words, those truths, when applied (that's a very important step you cannot skip!), will start to get rid of the toxins in your soul. The

Holy Spirit will help your spirit to begin the process of forgiving, loving and healing you in the physical and soul realms.

Instead of depression, you will live in joy, instead of anxiety, you will live in peace, instead of living in fear, you will live in God's love for you. The Word of God, when *activated* in your life, has the power to overcome anything that has come against you! You begin to live a new life, one empowered and governed by Holy Spirit.

When you live by the Spirit of God in you, your mind is renewed, your emotions follow (become more positive and life-giving), and your will desires to surrender to God and all His goodness.

That's how Jesus works to restore you from the inside out. **The "inside" of you, governed by Holy Spirit, becomes stronger and has the power to change you from being a person who's been living from the effects and circumstances of their "outside"/physical life into a brand-new person who is living from the "inside"/Spirit of God!**

As your spirit is reborn of God, it will become increasingly stronger in Jesus and it will have dominion over your physical life as well. You'll see a tangible difference in your home, your relationships, your workplace, your school, your finances, your body and more. **You will no longer be bound and defeated by what's going on on the outside because Holy Spirit will be working with you to help you overcome from the inside.**

The physical does not need to dominate who you are on the inside. You are loved, you are valued, and you are an overcomer through Christ Jesus.

Let's work through it...

> ▷ *How can you allow the Holy Spirit to take all the negative that happened to you in the physical realm and turn it around for the good for you?*
> ▷ *What does it look like for you to apply the Word of God to your thoughts so that your emotions and your will align with it?*

▷ *How can you allow the Holy Spirit to work to heal you from the inside out—from your spirit to your physical life?*

▷ *How can you stop the enemy from working from the outside to destroy your life?*

WHAT DOES TRUE TRANSFORMATION LOOK LIKE FOR YOU?

16

THE GOAL: DON'T PITCH A TENT THERE

———

"Not even GOD can change your past."

I've had many conversations over the years in which people have told me, "But you don't know my past. You don't know what I've done. I was an idiot. I made so many mistakes. I wish I could go back and change it. How can I possibly move forward? How could God possibly use me? God couldn't have plans for *my* life."

We *all* have a past. We all have a story. Some may be worse than others, but we all have something we've done or that's happened to us that we're disappointed about or ashamed of. There's nothing to change that. So why dwell on what's negative?

Without trying to sound insensitive, I want to ask you this question: **"You wanna pitch a tent *there*?"** I don't mean to be uncompassionate, but the truth of the matter is, you can't go back there. You can't undo the past. It's the past. But you can free yourself from it and make the choice to move forward into the future God has for you. It's your choice.

Do you want to move forward from your past, or have you decided that's the hill you're going to die on?

Have you thought of this next point before? Not even God Himself could change your past. That's right: God, in all His sovereignty, cannot change your past. Even if He wanted to, He couldn't because the past is the past. It's gone. It's not where you are now.

I'm sorry it happened. But it's in the PAST. Hear me: you are no longer *there*. You have moved into the present, whether you've noticed or not. **Your thoughts may still be in the past, but you live in the here and now with a choice to move into a better future.** Believe it or not, you are in control of what you want to live in and what you want to live for.

Your past does not define who you are today. God does not define who you are from your past. Your past may have influenced some of your choices today. Your past may have contributed to who you are today, but that doesn't mean you're still supposed to *live* in the past.

If anything from the past is immobilizing you from moving forward, God will help you through it to bring about change in your life. **But you've got to *want to* leave that place. You've got to pack up your tent and start on a new journey with Jesus.** He wants to do a new thing in your life. You don't want to miss it, do you?

> Forget the former things;
> > do not dwell on the past.
> See, I am doing a new thing!
> > Now it springs up; do you not perceive it?
> I am making a way in the wilderness
> > and streams in the wasteland. (Isaiah 43:18–19 NIV)

God wants to do a new thing in your life! In order to grab hold of the *new* that He has for you, you have to let go of the old, of the past. God will use things of the past to work His healing in and through you, but He doesn't want you to make your home in the past.

Think about it this way: if you can't leave the past in the past, how can you live for Jesus *today*? How can you fulfill all He asks of you *today*? If you carry baggage from the past, how can you run the race to fulfill your calling in the future? Carrying bags or baggage from a past trip is heavy. Your back hurts. It's a heavy load to always carry around. You may take it off every now and then and take a few minutes to sit and stretch without all that heavy weight on you, but you can't seem to part from those bags, or you just may not want to. **You've gotten used to carrying them. Those old bags belong to you. They're part of you. What would you do without them?**

Think about this. If you get rid of them, you may experience freedom! You just might start feeling better about yourself. You won't feel as heavy or burdened. You can walk faster, easier! You can run freely! How good does that sound to you?

I love these next scriptures. I pray they will encourage you to drop the weight of the past and move forward with Jesus. There is so much to be had in Him!

> ....let us strip off every weight that slows us down, especially the sin that so easily trips us up. And let us run with endurance the race God has set before us. We do this by keeping our eyes on Jesus, the champion who initiates and perfects our faith. (Hebrews 12:1–2 NLT)

> I admit that I haven't yet acquired the absolute fullness that I'm pursuing, but I run with passion into his abundance so that I may reach the purpose that Jesus Christ has called me to fulfill and wants me to discover. I don't depend on my own strength to accomplish this; however I do have one compelling focus: I forget all of the past as I fasten my heart to the future instead. I run straight for the divine invitation of reaching the heavenly goal and gaining the victory-prize through the anointing of Jesus. (Philippians 3:12–14 TPT)

The only way for you to begin living a new life with Jesus is to pack up your tent, leave the old baggage behind and begin taking steps in moving forward. Take one step at a time, one decision, one choice at a time, and soon you'll see how far you've come! While you walk forward, don't look back. Don't get caught up with "I should've, could've, and why didn't I?" questions. **Purpose in your heart to think and say, "I will, I can, and I'm going to make it!"** With God's help, you will learn to walk steadily towards all the *new* He has for you. And then, at times, you may even find yourself enjoying and running with full speed into His fields of grace for you!

Accepting God's Forgiveness

If you have confessed your sins to God, then you are forgiven! If you have truly repented from all the wrong you've done and are walking a different path with God, then you are truly forgiven. When God forgives, He does it for real, and He does not and will not bring it up again. The scriptures below are His promises to you about this.

You cannot ask God to forgive you and continue to beat yourself up or refuse His forgiveness because you feel guilty or ashamed. **If you are willing to move past it and move forward, then you must accept God's forgiveness for you and not live in the shadow of your sins anymore.**

You might be saying, "But because of my sin, I now am living with the consequences—so how can I not continue to be reminded of it and not let it get to me?"

Those consequences are the facts of your situation, but they are not the truth for you to live by. Let me explain: The fact is you sinned and have reaped its consequence, but the truth (that sets you free) is that God takes what was meant for evil against you, and He turns all things for the good for those who love Him (Romans 8:28). He makes all things new. Do not consider the things of old because He is doing a new thing (Isaiah 40.)

> For as high as the heavens are above the earth, so great is His loving devotion for those who fear Him. As far as the east is from the west, so far has He removed our transgressions from us. As a father has compassion on his children, so the LORD has compassion on those who fear Him. (Psalm 103:11–12 BSB)

Otherwise, He would have had to suffer repeatedly since the foundation of the world. But now He has appeared once for all at the end of the ages to do away with sin by the sacrifice of Himself. (Hebrews 9:26 BSB)

Then David said to Nathan, "I have sinned against the LORD." "The LORD has taken away your sin," Nathan replied. "You will not die." (2 Samuel 12:13 BSB)

Then I acknowledged my sin to You and did not hide my iniquity. I said, "I will confess my transgressions to the LORD," and You forgave the guilt of my sin. Selah (Psalm 32:5 BSB)

Surely, for my welfare I had such great anguish; but Your love has delivered me from the pit of oblivion, for You have cast all my sins behind Your back. (Isaiah 38:17 BSB)

I, yes I, am He who blots out your transgressions for My own sake and remembers your sins no more. (Isaiah 43:25 BSB)

Let's work through it…

My first questions for you to consider are rhetorical: If God can't change your past, why bother living in it? What are the benefits of spending so much of your precious time, thoughts and energy rehashing and allowing the past to ruin your present and your future?

You are so much more than your past and what happened there. It's a new day. God's mercies for you are new every morning! There is hope in Jesus, and there's much joy to be found in Him.

  ▷   *What do you need to leave in the past?*
  ▷   *What would it look like for you to pack up your tent and start walking forward?*
  ▷   *What are some things you're dreaming of doing in your future?*

HOW CAN YOU TRUST GOD TO LEAD YOU INTO A NEW LIFE?

SECTION 4

Building the Right Way

Goals:

- ▸ Be the little pig that built solid
- ▸ Stay committed to the Potter

BE A GIVER

17

THE GOAL: BE THE LITTLE PIG THAT BUILT SOLID

———

To get a good, solid life going, you need to answer this question honestly: **What have you been building your life on?**

Consider the story of "The Three Little Pigs." It's a fable about three pigs who built each of their houses out of three different materials. One house was made of hay. Another was made of sticks. The final house was made of bricks. The big bad wolf came and blew down the houses made of hay and sticks, completely destroying them. But he was unable to blow down and destroy the house made of bricks.

Hmm… Sounds a little like a story in the Bible that Jesus told. Let's take a look at that one, too:

> Therefore everyone who hears these words of mine and puts them into practice is like a wise man who built his house on the rock. The rain came down, the streams rose, and the winds blew and beat against that house; yet it did not fall, because it had its foundation on the rock. But everyone who hears these words of mine and does not put them into practice is like a foolish man who built his house on sand. The rain came down, the streams rose, and the winds blew and beat against that house, and it fell with a great crash. (Matthew 7:24–27 NIV)

It's interesting that the big bad wolf couldn't blow down the house made of bricks. Brick and rock are similar. They are solid, concrete substances, strong and hard to blow over. It is much more expensive to build with brick than just mere hay or sticks, but it is totally worth it. **I bet the pigs whose houses were blown down by the big bad wolf wished they would have invested in more valuable materials to build their houses with, like their third piggy-sibling did.** When their houses blew over, they lost *everything!* How sad, discouraging and frightening.

The Rock is solid

As a believer in and follower of Jesus Christ, you know that Jesus is THE ROCK on which you are to build your life if you want to withstand the storms throughout your time here on this earth. Through His Word, Jesus gives you wisdom and the tools to build your life on a *solid* foundation. He is the Rock which you build on, and He is strong. He is sure. He is steady and immovable. **If you build on Him, while you might be swayed in the windstorms of life, you won't be blown over.** It may feel like you have been at times, but the truth is that He never leaves you or forsakes you. He always makes a way for you. His Word is truth. He brings hope and light and life. In His Word, He provides everything you need to live a godly, abundant life.

Relying and living on human intellect, talents, position, power, status or wishful thinking is like building your life out of hay and sticks. When the "big bad wolf" comes around to blow it down, it will be blown down. Hay and sticks cannot withstand a strong blow from the enemy. Just like you read in the story above from the Gospel of Matthew, in order for your house not to fall apart when the enemy comes around to blow it down, you must build on the Word of God—on Jesus Christ Himself.

In the beginning was the Word, and the Word was with God, and the Word was God. (John 1:1 NIV)

For the word of God is alive and active. Sharper than any double-edged sword, it penetrates even to dividing soul and spirit, joints and marrow; it judges the thoughts and attitudes of the heart. (Hebrews 4:12 NIV)

God wants you to live by His Word. It is alive and active when you allow it to breathe into every area of your life. When you allow it to transform your thoughts and guide your actions, you build a solid foundation and good, strong walls. The Word of God helps you to see what needs fixing in your heart. It helps you change the way you think. It confirms and affirms how real He is and who you are when you are in Him.

The love of God gives you a life of peace and strength no matter what comes your way. His promises are sure, and you can count on them. Building your life on His love is wise, and it will give you the stability to stand when you are weak. His love is unconditional, full of mercy, wisdom, strength, truth, honor and life. There is no better foundation to build a life on.

The enemy (that big, bad wolf) comes to deceive you and ultimately wants to blow your house over. If you don't know, understand and receive the deep, unconditional love of God for you, the enemy is going to be able to mess with your life. You must be aware of his plans for your life. That may sound strange, but just as you know that God has plans for your life, the enemy has plans for your life, too. John 10:10 tells us that the thief comes to steal, kill and destroy you. Make no mistake: He is a thief and a liar!

In 1 Peter 5:8, God warns us: "Be alert and of sober mind. Your enemy the devil prowls around like a roaring lion looking for someone to devour" (NIV).

Doesn't that sound a lot like the big bad wolf? **But this enemy is not a character from a make-believe fable. He's all too real. You must be aware of his schemes.** My purpose in emphasizing this point is not to glorify the enemy. It's to help you understand that although God has great plans for your life and He loves you more than you can ever imagine, the enemy wants to discourage you and steal all God has for you. You must be alert and wise to that.

Jesus knew this was going to happen. It happened even in the time He walked with His own disciples. The enemy always tried to trip Him and His disciples up every chance he had. **That's why He gave his disciples (and us, today, who are His disciples) the answer and empowerment of His authority against the enemy.**

It's found in Luke 10:19—

> I have given you authority to trample on snakes and scorpions and to overcome all the power of the enemy; nothing will harm you. (NIV)

(*Snakes and scorpions* here mean a lot of things, but most importantly they mean schemes of the enemy that would cause you harm.)

The answer to defeating the enemy and to protecting your "house" against him is found in the love the Father has for you and in the authority of His Word to you. **Knowing that God loves you and has provided His authority to you against the enemy is key for your life not to fall apart!**

What's in your toolbox?

In the fifth chapter of the book of Galatians and throughout His Word, you will find the valuable tools to build your life on Some of the tools He provides for building a solid life are truth, peace, hope, faith, love, confidence, forgiveness, patience, kindness, goodness, self-control, joy, honesty, integrity, excellence... and the toolbox overflows! —principles, instructions, strategies and wisdom. **Open up this amazing toolbox (the Word) that He's provided, and you'll find no "tool" lacking and all you need to build strong.** It's all in there—no excuses not to be able to build solid! But you've got to use them!

Jesus has given us His authority to overcome the enemy in our lives. But the authority given to us only comes through *relationship* with Him.

And that's not knowing just *about* Him; it's *knowing* Him personally and being loved by Him. It's living with Him daily and authentically. He doesn't just give out His authority to strangers. He gives those who have a personal relationship with Him His authority. He gives His authority to those who are surrendered to His Lordship and who choose to follow Him.

Right from the beginning, He has proven His love for you is dependable and trustworthy. Jesus went through with the plan to lay down His life for you so that you can live in truth and freedom. That is the solid foundation from which you can begin to trust Him.

> You, dear children, are from God and have overcome them, because the one who is in you is greater than the one who is in the world. (1 John 4:4 NIV)

If you build your life on the Word of God, the Solid Rock, then the enemy has no chance of blowing your life down. He may try, but He won't succeed!

Let's work through it...

- ▷ *What foundation have you been building your life on?*
- ▷ *Has the enemy tried to "blow your house down?" What did that look like?*
- ▷ *What "materials" are you aware of that you can build a stronger life with?*

WHAT OTHER OR MORE TOOLS DO YOU NEED TO PICK FROM HIS TOOLBOX THAT CAN HELP YOU BUILD YOUR LIFE MORE SOLID?

18

THE GOAL: STAY COMMITTED
TO THE POTTER

———

I don't understand why I'm going through this. Why is God allowing this to happen to me? I'm too messed up. I'm too heartbroken. I don't think God could even put the pieces back together! What can I do to fix this—me?

My response? **God wastes nothing.** He is an artist who knows His creation so well that after He is done with it, all see its beauty. More than once in scripture, we see God compared to a potter and his people compared to clay. Consider these two passages.

> Yet you, LORD, are our father.
>> We are the clay, you are the potter:
>> we are all the work of your hand. (Isaiah 64:8 NIV)

So I went down to the potter's house, and I saw him working at the wheel. But the pot he was shaping from the clay was marred in his hands; so the potter formed it into another pot, shaping it as seemed best to him.

Then the word of the LORD came to me. He said, "Can I not do with you, Israel, as this potter does?" declares the LORD. "Like clay in the hand of the potter, so are you in my hand, Israel. (Jeremiah 18:3–6 NIV)

The Potter's wheel

A potter's wheel fascinates me. The clay and the potter have to work together. The potter molds, presses and handles the clay while spinning the wheel, all in an intentional manner, to create the finished product that he has in mind. He knows what he's making and how to do it. He knows what the finished product needs to look like. **And as long as that clay is in the skilled potter's hands, it *will* become the product the potter had in mind for it to be.**

That's what happens when we are growing in Christ. He is the Potter and we are the clay.

The following description of pottery provides a great picture of what we, as the clay, are made up of and how we can be molded and remade. It's also a clear description of what God, as the Potter, does with us as the clay in His hands. Take note how the physical explanation of the process is quite similar to how God makes us on the inside into the person He's created us to be.

Pottery is clay that is modeled, dried, and fired, usually with a glaze or finish, into a vessel or decorative object. Clay is a natural product dug from the earth, which has decomposed from rock within the earth's crust for millions of years. Decomposition occurs when water erodes the rock, breaks it down, and deposits them. It is important to note that a clay body is not the same thing as clay. Clay bodies are clay mixed with additives that give the clay different properties when worked and fired; thus pottery is not made from raw clay but a mixture of clay and other materials.

The potter can form his product in one of many ways. Clay may be modeled by hand or with the assistance of a potter's wheel, may be jiggered using a tool that copies the form of a master model onto a production piece, may be poured into a mold and dried, or cut or stamped into squares or slabs. The methods for forming pottery is as varied as the artisans who create them.

Pottery must be fired to a temperature high enough to mature the clay, meaning that the high temperature hardens the piece to enable it to hold water. An integral part of this firing is the addition of liquid glaze (it may be painted on or dipped in the glaze) to the surface of the unfired pot, which changes chemical composition and fuses to the surface of the fired pot. Then, the pottery is called vitreous, meaning it can hold water.[3]

Sometimes being on the Potter's wheel hurts. The words *dried, cut, molded, formed, fired,* etc., can be frightening in the thought process of what the Potter has to do to get the product to look a certain way to serve a certain purpose. It sounds like a lot of serious and detailed work, and it probably is. But if the Master Potter is working it, you can trust him. He's been doing it for a while now, with many people, for many purposes. You can trust that it will turn out exactly as it needs to. I think you get the picture, the analogy of what's happening to you. Being cut, molded, refined, and put into the fire is all about maturing and growing in His ways, as He burns and cuts off all that's not part of His original design for you to reflect His image, not yours. I'm not saying it's fun, but it's necessary if you truly want to live the life you were created to live. Without allowing the Potter to work on us, to remake us along the way, we won't be able to live out our purposes as effectively or even at all.

We need to surrender to His working in us in order for our lives to change. Nothing will change if change doesn't happen! Change to help you move forward is good. Change to help you grow more mature is good. We need to stop fighting being changed. If a caterpillar never went through its metamorphosis stage, it would never turn into the butterfly it was originally created to become. **Sometimes there's a struggle in the cocoon while it's waiting to change, but the change is worth the struggle!**

Be patient

I have found that the more I complain, argue, mumble and grumble during the process of being on the Potter's wheel, the longer the process.

---

[3] Nancy EV Bryk, "Pottery," How Products Are Made, accessed April 2, 2020, http://www.madehow.com/Volume-4/Pottery.html.

I get more anxious, angry, dissatisfied and am not pleasant to be around. Have you ever felt like this?

I feel as if the growing process isn't going fast enough. Or, I question: why do I even have to change in this area? Why can't I settle in just this one area? And my list of complaints goes on and on. Imagine a toddler who has to sit in his chair to finish his dinner. He squirms and cries and throws his food across the table, all because he's had enough of being in that high chair, belted down and forced to eat his food. He'd rather go play. I get that! I'm that toddler who just can't wait to get out of that high chair and be free of all restrictions to get to do what I want to do—now!

But there is a time and an order for everything. God created the world in six days and on the seventh He rested. **He had a strategic plan for how He was going to create everything, and it worked.** He has a strategic plan for how to shape you and mold you into becoming the awesome you He originally had in mind. For you, and for me, it's a matter of trust and a matter of patience.

I'm so thankful that I have a Father, a *good* Father who doesn't let go of me until He's done with the process for my good. He sees the end from the beginning. **He knows what it's going to take to get me ready for what's to come.** He knows what's missing in me and how to get it into me. He knows the places where I'm cracked and need putting back together. He knows me. He created me. He sees me and He hears me, and boy am I glad He has patience with me to make all things work together for the good for me—if I would only let Him without all my complaining and wrestling matches I get into with Him!

If I can only be patient with Him as He is with me. He loves me so much, and He loves you, too—enough to sometimes have to ignore your pleas to get out of that high chair. **He loves you enough to ignore your demands about how you think He should make you whole again**. In order to be patient with how the Potter is remaking you or with understanding the new designs He is creating for and within you, sometimes you must simply wait with quiet confidence and trust in Him. It sometimes means that you wait calmly while you may be feeling the fire or the cuts He puts you through. I want to encourage you (and me!) to be patient and look expectantly toward the absolute masterpiece He's creating in you. I don't think you will be disappointed.

Let God put you back together

Sometimes it seems as though you have shattered into a million pieces. How could all the pieces ever be put back together? It seems impossible! Or maybe, you think, those pieces were so horrible that not even God would want to use them to recreate you. These thoughts can lead you to think it's absolutely impossible for God to put you back together! You may fear that you aren't perfect enough or wanted enough by the Master Potter. Feelings of sadness, shame or regret mark your vessel. You try to paint over them with good works or better behavior, but the cracks where you've fallen apart always show up. The vessel doesn't seem to feel secure as feelings of bitterness or unforgiveness or unworthiness leak through. You may think, *What a mess I am!* But you are not. Only God can take the shattered pieces and do something beautiful with them. **There is nothing beyond God's ability or reach that can keep Him from restoring the most horrible, devastating or ugly things that have happened to you and make them into the most useful, most powerful and most effective tools in your life.** God is bigger than any evil or hurt that has come against you.

I will say it again: God wastes NOTHING! Like a professional potter, He knows how to take a cracked piece of clay and reform it into a useful piece again.

But we've got to trust Him.

He can remold the challenges, defeats, mistakes, and ugly things that have brought cracks and brokenness to our lives. He uses and remakes what's misshapen or broken and turns them into something lovely, useful and unique. He is always working to form us into His *original design*. He is always working to make us to look like Him.

When we are convinced without a shadow of a doubt that He truly loves us, then we are able to fully trust Him with what He is doing with us.

Let's work through it...

- ▷ *How can you trust that God knows you better than you know yourself and that He knows what He's doing with you?*
- ▷ *Are you on the Potter's wheel right now? Or in the fire? What is God saying to you in that?*
- ▷ *How does arguing and complaining against what God needs to do in and through you sabotage your life?*
- ▷ *How can you be more patient during the process of being remade, restored or refined by God?*

THE PROCESS IS NOT SIMPLE, BUT THE FINAL PRODUCT? IT WILL BE BEAUTIFUL, UNIQUE, USEFUL AND VALUABLE!

19

THE GOAL: BE A GIVER!

I hear so many people say that they don't have anything to give yet that is one of the most beautiful things we can do – to give to others. God is a giver. Why is this so important to know in your life? Understanding this can change your life. It can change the person you are. I've seen it change broken relationships and restore them again. **It takes the focus off of you and creates something powerful through you.** It can transform you from being a major worrier or being self-centered into being a generous, joy-filled person!

No more whining, worrying and complaining that you don't have what it takes. Or that you don't have enough to make it through, or that you don't have anything to give, or that you won't succeed, etc.! God is a giver and gives you good things without holding back from you.

> His divine power has given us everything we need for a godly life through our knowledge of him who called us by his own glory and goodness. (2 Peter 1:3 NIV)
>
> …[T]he Lord God formed a man from the dust of the ground and breathed into his nostrils the breath of life, and the man became a living being. (Genesis 2:7 NIV)

When God created Adam from the dust, He breathed His very own spirit into Adam, and Adam became a living being. Think about that for a long minute. **God gave Adam breath – His breath of life!** We have the very Spirit of God, who created the universe, inside of us… And we think we don't have what we need?! All we need is His spirit: the rest flows from that. And what flows from that can be very powerful and life-changing both for ourselves and others.

The passage in Matthew 6:25–34 is encouraging all the way through, but let's park on a seemingly small detail from it for a moment. **Did you know that God loves you more than a bird?**

> Look at all the birds—do you think they worry about their existence? They don't plant or reap or store up food, yet your heavenly Father provides them each with food. Aren't you much more valuable to your Father than they? So, which one of you by worrying could add anything to your life? (Vv. 26–27 TPT)

Birds do not worry about their existence. Do you hear that? Do I hear that? We are so prone to worrying—about everything. Worry kills faith. Worry kills motivation. Worry kills relationships. Worry is a killer, but God is a giver! If you have everything you need, then it doesn't make sense to worry, does it? God knows that. That's why He tells us in scripture that we are much more valuable than birds. If He provides for them, what can He not do for you?

God is a GIVER of life. **God gives us everything we need to successfully do this thing called life.** Everything we need physically, spiritually and emotionally? He's got it!

John 3:16 shows us just how much of a giver He is: "For God so loved the world that he GAVE his one and only Son…" (NIV, emphasis mine). If He gave His Son Jesus for you, do you not think He could provide all else you need?

What do you need? You need love? God is love and He gave Himself to you. You need peace? He is peace. He calms your storms. He gives you peace the world can never give you. You need comfort? He is your comforter. You need provision? He is your provider.

You need freedom? He is your rescuer. He is everything you need and more!

Begin to be a giver!

Many of us live feeling unfulfilled because we are not givers: we are worry-ers. But we are made in His image and if God is a giver, guess what? We are made to be givers, too. So, stop worrying about your own life and start giving. **Start reaching out and pouring into others what God has given you.**

It's like this: when you breathe in, you must breathe out. Since God breathed His Spirit into you, you now get to breathe it back out. What did He breathe into you when He breathed His Spirit? Love, peace, strength, goodness, joy, mercy: in other words, everything He is. This is the empowering picture I get every time I think of when God breathed into Adam. He became a living being. Before God breathed into him, Adam was lifeless. He wasn't able to receive, nor was he able to give. He was just—lifeless. He needed God's spirit to make him alive! We need God's spirit to make us alive! People need God's spirit to cause them to go from darkness to light, from sickness to health, from hopeless to hope-filled! Do you see how important it is to receive and to give of the goodness of God? All He is is good, and He gives us good things. We have the opportunity to give good things, too. We have this resource— the love and kindness of God. It's always available and it never runs out, not for anyone.

What does that mean for us today? **His Spirit gives us life so we can breathe that life into others.**

Stop complaining and worrying about what you don't have and focus on what you do have. **Reach into God's reservoir of goodness and fill yourself up so that He can overflow out of you!** Count your blessings. Share your blessings and stop whining about what you wish you had. As long as you continue to complain, compare and envy others, you will live a miserable life. Quit being ungrateful and start being thankful. You will see how fulfilling life will be when you do that. Focus on the blessings you do have and the blessing that you are. Determine to give from what you have. Take notice of the people in your life and the people who cross your path and ask the Lord what you can give to them. Stop worrying about what you don't have to give or what you are not.

Giving cures selfishness

Sometimes selfishness or fear can stop us from giving to others. We may not want to be inconvenienced, or we may not want to risk being rejected. That kind of attitude causes us to put the focus on ourselves instead of allowing God to shine in these opportunities. When we give, it helps us to be kinder, more loving, less judgmental and more compassionate. Giving causes us to experience the heart of our Father God. That's who He is, so that is who we are too. **Giving is not for our own gain: rather, it is more blessed to give than to receive.** We can change a person's whole life by our giving. We can give more love, more kindness, more patience, more time etc… What does God want you to give to others that will change you? That could change your relationships? That will impact your peers or your friends at work or school? What is God calling you to give?

The story in Acts 3 that changes lives

One day Peter and John were going up to the temple at the time of prayer—at three in the afternoon. Now a man who was lame from birth was being carried to the temple gate called Beautiful, where he was put every day to beg from those going into the temple courts. When he saw Peter and John about to enter, he asked them for money. Peter looked straight at him, as did John. Then Peter said, "Look at us!" So the man gave them his attention, expecting to get something from them.

Then Peter said, "Silver or gold I do not have, but what I do have I give you. In the name of Jesus Christ of Nazareth, walk." Taking him by the right hand, he helped him up, and instantly the man's feet and ankles became strong. He jumped to his feet and began to walk. Then he went with them into the temple courts, walking and jumping, and praising God. When all the people saw him walking and praising God, they recognized him as the same man who used to sit begging at the temple gate called Beautiful, and they were filled with wonder and amazement at what had happened to him. (Acts 1–10 NIV)

Peter and John didn't have anything physical to help this man, but they gave Him what they *did* have! The best they could give was the compassion and love of Jesus, and that manifested that day in His healing power that changed his life forever! Could you even imagine that moment? Peter and John didn't even have to stop to acknowledge this lame man. They could have been on their merry way to check off their own to-do list. But they took the time to stop. They reached deep into the endless resources of God's goodness and gave the lame man what he needed. They stopped, listened and obeyed the voice of Holy Spirit that day. They gave even when they could have made the excuse that they had nothing to give. What kindness! What generosity of God's goodness they shared!

Whatever you have to give, give it! When you do, you will see how beautiful you made someone's day—or life, for that matter.

You were created to be a giver of life because that's what your heavenly Father is! Look at just a few scriptures that show you what He has given to you.

For God has not given us a spirit of fear, but of power and of love and of a sound mind. (2 Timothy 1:7 NKJV)

By his divine power, God has given us everything we need for living a godly life. We have received all of this by coming to know him, the one who called us to himself by means of his marvelous glory and excellence. (2 Peter 1:3 NLT)

See what great love the Father has lavished on us, that we should be called children of God! And that is what we are! […] (1 John 3:1 NIV)

[Y]et for us there is but one God, the Father, from whom all things came and for whom we live; and there is but one Lord, Jesus Christ, through whom all things came and through whom we live. (1 Corinthians 8:6 NIV)

You can do this!

You are strong in Him:

I can do all things through Christ who strengthens me. (Philippians 4:13 NIV)

You are God's handiwork, created for purpose:

For we are God's handiwork, created in Christ Jesus to do good works, which God prepared in advance for us to do. (Ephesians 2:10 NIV)

Let's work through it…

You have been given so much through God's love for you, and you have so much to give back out because of Him.

> ▷ *Why and how can you trust God to meet your every need?*
> ▷ *What can you list that He has already given you that has blessed your life so far?*
> ▷ *How can you be a better giver? In your family? In your relationships? At work? At school? At church?*

How can you become bolder in your giving?

SECTION 5

Purposed to Serve

Goals:

- ▶ Get under His covering (Isaiah 61)
- ▶ Recognize and use what's in your hand
- ▶ Offer Him your lunch

SERVE WITH GRATITUDE, NOT ATTITUDE

20

THE GOAL: GET UNDER HIS COVERING

If you took the time to study the life of Jesus, you would find that everything He did—from spending time praying to the Father, ministering to the sick, delivering those oppressed and possessed of the devil, sharing the Good News with the poor, feeding the hungry and loving people where they were at—He was leaving an example of what *we* should also be doing. **To imitate Jesus and to continue to do what He did is an honorable call to each of His followers.** It is God's will for each of us. But before Jesus did what the Father told Him to do, He was filled with the Holy Spirit. Let's take a look at what that means:

> The Spirit of the LORD will rest on him—
>> the Spirit of wisdom and of understanding,
>> the Spirit of counsel and of might,
>> the Spirit of the knowledge and fear of the LORD. (Isaiah 11:2 NIV)

> …God anointed Jesus of Nazareth with the Holy Spirit and power, and… he went around doing good and healing all who were under the power of the devil, because God was with him. (Acts 10:38 NIV)

> …[T]he Holy Spirit descended on him in bodily form like a dove. And a voice came from heaven: "You are my Son, whom I love; with you I am well pleased." (Luke 3:22 NIV)

In Isaiah 61:1–3, Jesus shows us His calling and how He fulfilled the Father's plans for His life on earth.

> The Spirit of the Sovereign Lord is on me,
>   because the Lord has anointed me
>   to proclaim good news to the poor.
> He has sent me to bind up the brokenhearted,
>   to proclaim freedom for the captives
>   and release from darkness for the prisoners,
> to proclaim the year of the Lord's favor
>   and the day of vengeance of our God,
> to comfort all who mourn,
>   and provide for those who grieve in Zion—
> to bestow on them a crown of beauty
>   instead of ashes,
> the oil of joy
>   instead of mourning,
> and a garment of praise
>   instead of a spirit of despair.
> They will be called oaks of righteousness,
>   a planting of the Lord for
>   the display of his splendor. (NIV)

By His example, Jesus shows us how to live and how to honor the Holy Spirit that rests on us. It's His spirit of wisdom and understanding. It is the counsel of the Lord and the knowledge and the fear of God. It is with the spirit of great might. Jesus didn't just walk around the earth trying to figure out who, what and how. He was filled with the Holy Spirit who gave Him wisdom, direction, strength and all He needed to minister with. As He ministered to those around Him, His Holy Spirit was able to transform lives, healing them and setting them free from their bondage. The call is the same for us today. **He has passed on the baton to us: We get to work with Holy Spirit to continue and fulfill His great commission!**

To accomplish this, we need to be empowered by His love and His Holy Spirit.

And now I will send the Holy Spirit, just as my Father promised. But stay here in the city until the Holy Spirit comes and fills you with power from heaven. (Luke 24:49 NLT)

Let your light so shine before men, that they may see your good works, and glorify your Father which is in heaven. (Matthew 5:16 NKJV)

Jesus said to him, "You shall love the LORD your God with all your heart, with all your soul, and with all your mind." This is the first and great commandment. And the second is like it: "You shall love your neighbor as yourself." (Matthew 22:37–39 NKJV)

He said to them, "Go into all the world and preach the gospel to all creation. Whoever believes and is baptized will be saved, but whoever does not believe will be condemned. And these signs will accompany those who believe: In my name they will drive out demons; they will speak in new tongues; they will pick up snakes with their hands; and when they drink deadly poison, it will not hurt them at all; they will place their hands on sick people, and they will get well." (Mark 16:15–18 NIV)

The reason for this is that everyone would be reconciled back to God—through the Son, Jesus Christ. **You, as a believer in Jesus, have been given that ministry of reconciliation.** What an awesome privilege it is to see lives touched and transformed by the love of Jesus for all of eternity, all because you said, "Yes, Lord."

Now this is from God, who reconciled us to Himself through Christ and gave us the ministry of reconciliation: that God was reconciling the world to himself in Christ, not counting people's sins against them. And he has committed to us the message of reconciliation. (2 Corinthians 5:18–19 NIV)

It's the same HOLY SPIRIT, and it's the same calling!

Think about this for a minute: The same Holy Spirit that rests on YOU was upon Jesus, whom we just read about in Isaiah 61. The spirit of the

Sovereign Lord, His Holy Spirit, now resides in you to continue the work of the ministry. YOU have been commissioned to preach the good news to those who never heard it. That they would be saved for all of eternity! YOU have been anointed to bring the message of deliverance to those who are in captivity, those sitting in darkness crying out for help and hope! YOU have been given the message of joy to those who are in depression and despair.

Look around you. This world is in confusion. It's begging for a Redeemer, a Rescuer, to rescue us out of all the mess we are in. **You have the Holy Spirit within you to speak life, to speak empowerment and encouragement, to help lead the way to the only true Light that expels darkness.** No, *you* are not their Savior, but you have the privilege of pointing them to the Savior! You have the honor and the calling to allow the Holy Spirit to flow from you what they need from Him! You are a conduit of His love to those in need.

The baton gets passed on

Think about it. Jesus came. He passed the baton to His followers to do the same thing He did so that people would come to know Him, believe in Him, experience Him in their own personal lives and give Him the glory. Hopefully, those we get to minister to will, in turn, do the same: pick up the baton and minister to others they meet the same way Jesus did to them.

For the Spirit of the Sovereign Lord is upon *you*.... You can't do it by yourself. You need the help, the anointing, wisdom, guidance, strength of Holy Spirit to accomplish such a great calling. The Spirit of God who rests on you to fulfill the great commission is the same Spirit that rose Jesus from the dead! He is living in you today if you are a follower of Jesus. And He doesn't live in you for no reason—He lives in you for a purpose, and I believe it is found right there in Isaiah 61:1–3.

The Holy Spirit is the One who reminds us of all Jesus did. Why is this important? I believe so that we don't forget who Jesus is, why He came and how He lived. Jesus is the ultimate example of how we can be used to change lives. We must remember that if Jesus, while He lived as a man on this earth, needed the Holy Spirit to accomplish great things, so we too need the Holy Spirit in the same way!

Let's work through it…

- ▷ *How does the Holy Spirit rest on you?*
- ▷ *What does it mean to be anointed by the Holy Spirit?*
- ▷ *Why would you need the Holy Spirit to anoint you?*

IN REFERENCE TO ISAIAH 61:1–3, HOW IS GOD ALREADY USING YOU TO TOUCH PEOPLE'S LIVES OR HOW CAN YOU BEGIN TO BE USED BY GOD IN THIS WAY?

21

THE GOAL: RECOGNIZE AND USE WHAT'S IN YOUR HAND

———

Then the LORD asked him, "What is that in your hand?" "A shepherd's staff," Moses replied. (Exodus 4:2 NLT)

God showed Moses that He could use his ordinary staff to perform miracles as a sign for the unbelieving nations of Israel and Egypt. **As Moses' trust in God grew, God was able to take what was in Moses' hand and do unimaginable miracles that must have left Moses absolutely stunned!** I know I would be! If you take the time to read the book of Exodus, I believe you, too, will be at a loss for words at the extraordinary wonders performed with the ordinary object God used which was found in Moses' hand, his staff.

But that's what God does. He takes what's normal to us and is able to bring the divine and the supernatural to our lives and to the lives around us today. That's what is so exciting about giving God what we have "in our hand."

So what's in your hand? It's a clue to what God may be calling you to!

We each have a unique calling. We are called to accomplish the great plans God established for us. He had us in His heart from day one. He created and formed us for His purpose, put together a plan for us and wrote every day of our lives in His book for us before we lived even one day. Remember our previous look into Psalm 139?

> Your eyes saw my unformed body;
>> all the days ordained for me were written in your book
>> before one of them came to be. (v. 16 NIV)

That's how precious and cherished we are to Father God. He designed a plan just for us.

We have a calling to fulfill. But what does that even mean? And how can we know what it is?

We need to know this about ourselves: We weren't created just to exist or to be like everyone else (no one could be even if they tried). **We weren't created to just dream about having a meaningful life: He created us each to *be* a meaningful life.**

Think about it this way. We all possess skills, talents and strengths. Are you using all of yours? At least some? If you are, are you using them to impact the world around you? Are you bringing God's hope and love to others to impact their lives for eternity? Yes: for eternity. I don't just mean to impact lives here on earth just for the sake of doing good works here. No. I believe we are each called to use what God has given us to impact lives for eternity—to introduce Jesus to them that they might be with Him for eternity—their original dwelling place!

Is your life *reflecting* God? If it is, you're living out who you truly are, and you are bringing glory to HIM.

There's so much in you

If you think you don't have skills, talents or strengths to contribute, let me ask you: Really? God created the universe, put the stars in place and holds it and you together. Do you think He skipped over you and forgot to download skills, talents or strengths into you? He couldn't do that. **Everything God creates is complete, excellent and without mistake.**

That includes you. He downloaded His plan for you into you while you were still in your mother's womb.

End of discussion. He said it. It's truth.

> Every good thing given and every perfect gift is from above, coming down from the Father of lights, with whom there is no variation or shifting shadow. (James 1:17 NASB)

> For we are God's handiwork, created in Christ Jesus to do good works, which God prepared in advance for us to do. (Ephesians 2:10 NIV)

> Each of you should use whatever gift you have received to serve others, as faithful stewards of God's grace in its various forms. (1 Peter 4:10 NIV)

The verdict is… you are LOADED!

The verses above are only *some* of the scriptures which reveal that God gives us each gifts and skills to be used for Him. He created us with unique minds, hearts, and passions. **Only you can do what you can in the way you do it.** When you embrace all He's placed within you and submit it back to Him, He will open up opportunities for you to positively affect others' lives.

You are wise, you are compassionate, you are kind, you are courageous, you are strong, you are an influencer, you are full of joy, and you are full of hope! You look like your Father God, and you have His heart. His heart is for His love and power to be seen and felt by mankind. His will is that His love would reach people and bless them with His presence and goodness. His heart is for you to fulfill His purposes on the earth: to reach people in all areas of life through whatever He's put in your hands.

So with all of that, what are the skills and gifts He's placed in your hands? **What did He put in you that seems ordinary, but that once it's placed in God's hands, He could work the extraordinary with it?**

What is a "calling"?

Christians often think that a "calling" means becoming a missionary, going overseas, doing good things for the poor and preaching in little huts. If God wants you to be that sort of missionary and He's given you the gifts and tools for it, that's awesome! Go for it! But that's not everyone's calling.

While some are called to be missionaries, that picture of what you think is a calling can limit your perception and hinder you from fulfilling the calling God has for *you*. God expects our callings to be lived out in practical ways every day. **Are you matching your calling with the skills He's given you so that you can be that much more effective?** For example, if I can't sing and I am tone deaf, I shouldn't expect my calling to be a professional singer—and I shouldn't feel bad that it's not my calling. While you can be educated in a specific subject to work in that area, if you don't have the gift or the talent to be honed and sharpened in that area, you probably won't be very successful or very blessed in it. If I see blood and faint, I probably shouldn't try to become a surgeon. I think you get what I'm saying.

Moses used his staff

One way to begin to discover God's calling in your life is to recognize what He has put in your hands. What are your natural abilities and gifts? Those are God-given! Moses was a shepherd. Daily, he tended sheep. He did it well. He used what was in his hand as one of the most important and valuable tools for his job. He understood what he needed to be a successful shepherd. **He knew how to use his tool, and he used it well.** When he surrendered his calling as a shepherd and what was in his hand to God, the thing that was used in the natural and normal life of a shepherd became supernatural and divine. And with that, he was used mightily as a shepherd or leader of God to lead the nation of Israel out of Egypt. Wow! Who would have thought? I wonder if Moses ever thought about what or where he and his staff would end up?

What skills do you have? What areas of your life, work, and career match up? **Are you willing to give yourself and what you hold in your hand to God?** For His purposes? Would you be willing to let go of *your* thoughts and plans and put your trust in Him to take you where He needs you to be?

Remember, God works through you from the inside out, and He will use all of who He created you to be in the physical realm and in the spiritual realm together. Using all of who you are, His desire and great commission for you is that He is revealed through whatever you do.

Let's work through it...

Get practical about what you bring to the table.

This is something to think about: The gifts that God gives us are perfect. So it's not the gifts that need to be perfected, honed, developed etc... it is we who need to be perfected, honed, developed etc. to be able to exercise the gifts.

> ▷ *In what ways do you believe you need to grow to be able to handle and steward the perfect gifts that God has given you?*

Take a few minutes (or a few days) to think about what you're good at or passionate about. It's not prideful to do that. If you're skilled and strong in an area, it's good to work confidently in it. Doing so honors God because He gave you those skills, talents, abilities and strengths. When you're aware of what you bring to the table, you'll be more open to the opportunities before you to use what you have been given by God—or in other words, to work in your calling.

> ▷ *What am I passionate about? What am I good at?*
> ▷ *What practical steps can I take to continue to develop in those areas?*
> ▷ *How might these help me discover or work in my calling?*

WHAT WOULD IT TAKE FOR GOD TO TURN MY "ORDINARY" INTO "EXTRAORDINARY"?

22

THE GOAL: OFFER HIM YOUR LUNCH

He did what with that boy's lunch?

Do you know you can be an agent of change, even if what you have to offer seems small and insignificant?

To illustrate this, let's take a quick look at a famous Bible story. I'm not going to exegesis it all out for you. I don't have deep nuggets of hidden revelation about it. I just want to share a simple but powerful example of what being an agent of change is all about. **An agent of change is one who is willing to be used to change the norm, to change what's always been, to risk defying the old and to bring about something new: yes—even a miracle!** I believe Holy Spirit will show you yourself in this story, and He will show you what He wants to do in and with your life.

The story is simple but life-changing:

> When Jesus looked out and saw that a large crowd had arrived, he said to Philip, "Where can we buy bread to feed these people?" He said this to stretch Philip's faith. He already knew what he was going to do. Philip answered, "Two hundred silver pieces wouldn't be enough to buy bread for each person to get a piece."

One of the disciples—it was Andrew, brother to Simon Peter—said, "There's a little boy here who has five barley loaves and two fish. But that's a drop in the bucket for a crowd like this."

Jesus said, "Make the people sit down." There was a nice carpet of green grass in this place. They sat down, about five thousand of them. Then Jesus took the bread and, having given thanks, gave it to those who were seated. He did the same with the fish. All ate as much as they wanted.

When the people had eaten their fill, he said to his disciples, "Gather the leftovers so nothing is wasted." They went to work and filled twelve large baskets with leftovers from the five barley loaves.

The people realized that God was at work among them in what Jesus had just done. (John 6:5–15 MSG)

It may not be much, but it's something!

What an incredible story of faith and trust from an unnamed little boy who gave the very little—but all he had—to Jesus. **When he left his house that morning with the little lunch his mom must have made him, he had no idea what his lunch was going to become.**

Are you like the little boy? You may feel you don't have much "in your hand," that you don't have much to give to Jesus to work with. If that's true for you, you probably have *no idea* just what God can do with it if you would surrender it all to Him and believe... If you could believe that when you leave your house for the day, that you could be used in a miracle that will forever change a life—how amazing would that be? Is that even possible? Well, if it was for that little boy, then it could be true for you, too! With God, all things are possible, right? We've heard that a thousand times, but what if you really believed it about your own life and expected it? "Without faith it is impossible to please God" (Heb. 11:6 NIV). Can you imagine how pleased God is when we operate our daily lives in this kind of miracle-working faith?

Jesus takes the boy's lunch, blesses it (gives thanks), and then multiplies it. The boy's lunch provides food for *everyone* there. **That is what your gift in Jesus' hands is supposed to do, too: bless all those around you.** When you submit your gift to God, He can bless it and multiply it and accomplish His purposes through you. People's lives will be blessed when you give your gift (even if you think it's not enough) to God. To think: a little boy had something *Jesus* needed to feed the crowd. Once the people experienced God's miracle, they recognized it was Jesus who did that for them. They experienced His love. They acknowledged Him. All the glory goes to God, right? Because we can't do the miraculous on our own. That's the whole point: that the love and power of God would be seen throughout the earth—throughout our daily lives—through us! And through that, many will put their trust in *Him*.

When we live our lives daily like the little boy who gave his lunch did, amazing things can follow—even miracles, miracles we were not even looking for.

Giving to Jesus is part of our worship experience

In everything, you get to worship Him. In your calling, you get to worship Him. Through what God does with what's in your hands, you get to worship Him. In your gifts, you get to worship Him. That's the biggest joy and the greatest fulfillment anyone can experience – to worship Him!

It all boils down to being willing to be an agent of change. You can bring change to all sorts of people and situations, just like the little boy did. You can trust God with what you have. After all, He's the one who gave it to you in the first place. Would you give it all back to Him for the chance to change your world?

I love the end of this miracle when Jesus tells His disciples to gather up the leftovers, to not waste anything. As we saw with God as the Potter, God wastes nothing. Nothing of your life is ever wasted when God has His hand on it. And the leftovers? While your gifts, strengths, skills and abilities "feed" others, they also feed you. They feed you God's goodness and love for *you*. There is fulfillment for you when God uses you. He delights in that. **When you feed others with what's in your hand, God will make sure you're taken care of, too!**

I bet as Jesus watched the little boy's bread and fish multiply in His hands, He got a kick out of the expressions of awe, wonder, confusion and shock on everyone's faces, including the little boy's face. The little boy's eyes must have been HUGE when he witnessed his lunch multiplying! What a *wonder-full* miracle.

When you put all of what's in your hands into His hands, He will do *wonder-full* things in, through and for you.

Let's work through it...

- ▷ *What do you know that God put into you when He wove and knit you together in your mother's womb?*
- ▷ *Do you hesitate to give to Jesus what's in your hand? If so, why?*
- ▷ *How quick are you to obey Jesus and give Him all you have?*
- ▷ *Why do you think you sometimes hold on to even the little you have?*

WHAT DO YOU DREAM COULD HAPPEN IF JESUS TOOK WHAT YOU GAVE HIM AND BLESSED IT AND MULTIPLIED IT?

23

THE GOAL: SERVE WITH GRATITUDE, NOT ATTITUDE

———

That day the little boy gave his lunch, Jesus didn't just feed the crowd with physical food: He used it to show them His compassion and love. He didn't just meet their physical need for a meal for one day; He impacted their lives for eternity. He wanted them to know He valued them. They were important enough for Him to provide them what they needed. And that's what He desires for you: that you would allow Him to use you to touch the people around you, that they would know His compassion and love for them for eternity.

Ask yourself: "Do my family and friends feel loved and cared for by me? Or do I just serve them out of duty? What kind of an attitude do they get from me when I'm doing things for them? Do the people I am in school with or who I'm working with feel loved, cared for and valued by me?" Those are honest questions that deserve honest answers. If you don't care about them or you think they're not worth your time or kindness, you won't be a reflection of God at all, and they sure won't see His love for them through you.

Attitude while serving is important

Every time Jesus performed a miracle, it was because He had compassion and wanted to reflect the love of the Father. **If your attitude is one of**

kindness and love, your work and your service to others will reflect what's already in you—the heart of the Father. Others will see in your attitude and in your work something different, special or even just something *good*—that quality alone is remarkable.

Do you value people? Do you let them know they're important? Do you serve them as the disciples served the people in the following story?

Mark 6:38–44 recounts the story we just read in John 6 in a previous chapter. In the account in Mark, Jesus asks the disciples to go find food for 5,000 men and their families. That's quite a task, wouldn't you agree? After they bring Him the little they find, He asks them to have this massive group sit in small groups. I wonder how long that must have taken to organize? Talk about crowd control!

Finding the food then organizing the huge crowd into small groups was quite the challenge. Thousands of hungry, tired, sunburned men, women and children were asked to split up and sit down in their assigned circles. If that wasn't enough, then Jesus asked His disciples to distribute the food to each person there! Again, I can't even imagine how long that must have taken or how difficult that could have been. I mean, did Jesus multiply the food all at once, or did He do it as each group was fed? Did the disciples have a system in place? Was the crowd yelling for food? Were some of them rude? How do you accomplish such a task without "losing it"? I think by that time, if I were one of the disciples, I would have been tired, overwhelmed and maybe a bit irritated.

We really don't know what attitude the disciples had while they served the people, but they did it! I believe they loved and respected Jesus and wanted to please Him. I believe they were learning to obey Him and trusted that He knew what He was doing. I also believe the wonder of the miracle of multiplication was fascinating to them. But that's just my imagination. The fact is, they obeyed and served their Master, and a great need was met that day.

After all the people were fed, Jesus asked the disciples to do one more act of service—to gather up ALL the leftovers and put them in baskets.

Really, Lord? Couldn't the people just put their leftovers in doggie bags and take them home? But no, the disciples picked up twelve extra baskets with leftovers in them!

All kidding aside, I don't think the disciples could have been serving in a bad mood as they saw the miracle of multiplication keep taking place right before their very eyes. How exciting it must have been for everyone to see this miracle. Can you imagine the joy of it all?

Imagine with me again: there must have been so much buzz and excitement in the atmosphere. Can you hear the squeals of the children when the bread keeps appearing? Oh, what a day that must have been! I bet no one ever forgot it as long as they lived.

Serving Jesus and those hungry people must have been fulfilling. To see a need and be able to fill it leaves you feeling satisfied, doesn't it?

You may not personally experience such a grand miracle, but whatever Jesus asks you to do, how do you do it? What's your attitude in it? What is your motive? How do you feel after you've obeyed Him? What you're asked to do doesn't have to be on a grand scale. Sometimes it's the small things that impact someone's life for the good.

Do you take the time to talk to others and show them you care? Do you show them they're valued and are seen by God? **Are you willing to be used for the benefit of others?**

The example of an apple tree

When an apple tree bears fruit, it doesn't pick and eat its own fruit. It bears fruit for others to pick and eat. If people don't pick the apple from the tree when it's ripe, the apple will eventually fall off the branch and rot. It won't be edible, and its original purpose is gone.

If you believe your gifts and abilities are for *your* benefit, you're missing the point.

When others "eat of" your fruit (talents, skills, gifts…), they are better off somehow, some way because they taste the blessing of Jesus on your life. They'll never forget it.

If you are bearing the fruit of love and someone needs to be loved that day, can they pick that love off of you? Will you share that fruit of love with them? If someone needs the fruit of kindness that day, can they pick off the fruit of kindness from you? When I go apple picking, I'm so thankful for all the apple trees there are for me to pick off of! (Those apple desserts are delicious that I make from those apples I just picked!) Sometimes, they'll even ask what kind of fruit you're bearing and they will want to have a part of it. (They won't ask in those exact words, but that's really what they want to know.) That's where your opportunity to share the Gospel comes in. **No matter what you're doing as your calling, if you allow God to bless it and use it, people will be changed!**

You may be a stay-at-home mom: your gifts of love and discipline will shape, direct and encourage a child to be all God calls them to be. You may be a high school teacher or a church nursery care worker with the gifts of teaching and encouragement which will help a student believe in themselves. You may be a student with the gift of gab (I count myself as one who has that gift!), and your late-night talks will help other students persist through tough times when they want to quit.

> Work willingly at whatever you do, as though you were working for the Lord rather than for people. (Colossians 3:23 NLT)

> So whether you eat or drink or whatever you do, do it all for the glory of God. (1 Corinthians 10:31 NIV)

Serving can be challenging, but the results can be humbling and joyful! Let's be careful to serve with an attitude of gratefulness that God would choose you to bear fruit for others to enjoy.

Let's work through it...

You will never know how your gifts can be used to fulfill your calling to help change your world until you allow Him to use you whenever, however, and wherever. Start now by considering these questions.

▷ *What attitude do you have when serving others?*
▷ *Do you believe your gifts and service are effective?*
▷ *What fruit are you bearing?*
▷ *Are you allowing others to pick 'fruit' from you?*

HOW CAN YOU KNOW IF OTHERS SEE JESUS IN YOU?

Two Roadblocks You Need to Be Aware Of

Goals:

▶ Stop operating from a spirit of fear

KNOW THE FACTS BUT ACTIVATE THE TRUTH

24

THE GOAL: STOP OPERATING FROM A SPIRIT OF FEAR

———

God is love—He is perfect love—only He can cast out fear.

> So we have come to know and to believe the love that God has for us. God is love, and whoever abides in love abides in God, and God abides in him. […] There is no fear in love; but perfect love casts out fear, because fear involves torment. But he who fears has not been made perfect in love. (1 John 4:16,18 NKJV)

> For God has not given us a spirit of fear, but of power and of love and of a sound mind. (2 Timothy 1:7 NKJV)

I am always astounded to note how often we operate from a *spirit of fear* in our day-to-day lives.

Where did the spirit of fear come from?

In the garden story about Adam and Eve, we learn that it wasn't until *after* they sinned that they made clothes for themselves with fig leaves and ran away to hide. Why did they do that? We don't have to guess: Adam told God he was *afraid* and hid (Genesis 3:10).

Before sin, Adam never experienced fear. So back to the question of where did fear come from. Fear came in through sin and rebellion.

Sin produces fear in us. It's destructive and causes us to hide in shame, condemnation and regret. Fear immobilizes us from living free.

Fear is a tactic the enemy uses against the children of God. Only when we give in to the enemy and his lies (as Adam and Eve did) do we experience fear.

If we allow the spirit of fear to control us, we invite issues into our lives that could keep us bound for years.

Do you operate from this crippling spirit of fear in certain areas of your life?

The spirit of fear has many different faces. As I unpack a few of them, you might recognize it in your own life. If you do, invite Holy Spirit to free you from it.

Fear of success

Usually, we hear of people fearing failure—and we'll talk about that next. But as unlikely as it might sound, a fear of *success* is one of the biggest fears I help clients overcome. I call it the "Familiar blankie syndrome." A fear of success is usually *linked* to a fear of failure but it's success that's the issue here. It looks like this:

Picture a child dragging around his favorite blankie. He brings it with him everywhere he goes. If mom takes it away to wash it, this kid has a fit! The blankie is his comfort. It's *familiar*. If he is in a strange or foreign environment or place, but he has his blankie, all is well. He can adjust as long as he has his blankie.

The same scenario repeats itself for a person who has believed themselves to be a 'failure' most of their lives or chooses to live in a "less-than" way of life or environment. She is accustomed to 'failing' or to not having enough. *Less-than* is comfortable. She's always known it. Anything different puts her in a spin, and she's likely to eventually run from it. Even if she isn't productive or getting anywhere in life, or if she's being abused, bullied or demeaned by the people around her, she'll choose to stay there because that's all she knows. It's *familiar*. It's her blankie. She knows how to navigate it and survive. She knows what to expect and she knows what's expected of her (which is usually nothing or at least nothing good).

So, put her in a place of success—where she accomplishes something. Success is different. It's not familiar. It's new. It's not something she is used to. It feels good for a while, but eventually, success terrifies her. She doesn't know what to do with success. **In order to succeed and leave failure behind, she's had to take different steps, operate from different systems and ditch the old way of doing things.** She did all of that and succeeded. She let go of the familiar—the blankie. This is great, right?

Unfortunately, many in this hypothetical woman's situation don't know what to do with a new way of thinking, living or achieving accomplishments, and they adopt a fear of success. Success frightens them because in order to keep achieving and living at that level of success, they have to keep the bar higher than they've ever had it. They have to continue putting in work and maintain the necessary stamina to persevere in that success or to keep succeeding. The familiar at that point cannot be welcomed nor tolerated. For some, that's hard. Success must be sustained now. It's not familiar, nor is it comfortable. Many give up at this point and go back to what is familiar—failure. It's just easier. That familiar spirit will destroy you.

I'm sure you've heard stories of people who were homeless or in poverty who somehow became famous, got into a lot of money, and their lives changed for the better. Their stories seem inspiring until you realize you *aren't* hearing about them anymore. You find out that they're back on the streets, homeless and poor again.

Why does that happen? Frequently, they would rather live in what is familiar (even if it's not the best thing for them) than work hard, keep putting in the effort and keep pushing through towards a better, safer, healthier, more successful life.

It's disheartening to think that because being successful is scary or hard, you can come so far, leave behind old places of failure, despair and doubt, only to want to go back.

It's easy to live in a place of failure even if it's not where we want to be or what we want to live in. We tolerate it. This is usually because we don't believe how valuable we are in God's eyes and how truly loved we are by God or that God has good plans for us. This is why it is so important to grasp and know how truly valuable we are, how strong we really can be and that it is possible to move forward. When we know God has given us everything we need for success, it inspires us and gives us the courage to change. **But we need to let go of our familiar blankie and grow up and move on towards the better things God has for us.**

Fear of failure

Living in fear of failure can lead to an unhealthy lifestyle. Fear of failure can drive us to work until we drop. We may compromise our values and beliefs just so we don't risk getting left behind or someone else getting "there" before us. Fear of failure can dominate our sleep. We would rather lose sleep than not finish that project, or we work till all hours of the morning to get the job done. **When fear of failure causes us to compromise even our own health, we have a bigger problem than we know.** Fear of failure will often drive us to work hard, reach higher, make longer strides to get to the top, but all the while, we sabotage and risk our health, relationships and sanity. And for what? We will do whatever it takes and sacrifice whatever or whomever in our lives to make sure we never live life below the standards of what is deemed wealth, high position, or power. Fear of failure will drive wedges between husbands and wives, parents and children as they put goals to achieve success first above anyone or anything that might hold them back. This kind of hard work or perseverance is not healthy or Godly in any way. It actually demonstrates that we are our own god, and our success or lack of it is determined solely by what or who we are willing to sacrifice.

Is working hard and accomplishing goals a bad thing? No, not at all. But we should ask: what is our driving motive or force? Working hard and reaching success doesn't have to come at the cost of hurting the people around you or allowing yourself to become obsessed with that lifestyle. Fear of failure can invoke the spirit of greed. Someone in this situation must be careful to discern what is driving them at all times. Is it really worth losing your family, your faith in God or your health for money, position and power? All of that could go away in a moment. Then what are you left with? Unfortunately, nothing but heartbreak, disappointment, anger and a whole bunch of other negative consequences will weigh in.

Work hard, meet goals—but honor God and others while you're doing it.

So many fears...

Fear of not being good, smart, popular or liked enough can also cause you to stay stuck right where you are. That's a lie. Only the truth can counteract that.

Let's look at some scriptures that will help you to kick that spirit of fear out of your life! God cares about this very real issue of fear you deal with, so He provides you with equipping and empowering truths. Learn them, believe them, apply them, and watch fear begin to grow smaller and smaller in those areas of your life!

2 Timothy 1:7 says that "God has not given us a spirit of fear, but of power and of love and of a sound mind" (NKJV). That spirit of fear is never given to us by God. **When you have God's love living in you, His authority backing you up and a disciplined mind that is at peace, the spirit of fear has no place in you!** THIS is the victory God has given you over the spirit of fear!

1 John 3:1 says, "See what great love the Father has lavished on us, that we should be called children of God" (NIV). He has given us love. We talked quite a bit about God's unconditional, never-ending love He has for each one of us. He's given His love to us so that we would not have to

live in fear. When you know Whose you are, there is no reason to fear! Do you know Whose you are? You are the child of the Almighty God who created the Heavens and the Earth! That's Whose you are! So in the light of that fact, can fear really win?

Luke 10:19 says, "I have given you authority to trample on snakes and scorpions and to overcome all the power of the enemy; nothing will harm you" (NIV). He has given us His name, His power and His authority over the schemes and plans of the enemy. **His authority backs us up in the face of fear!** Because He already defeated the enemy, the spirit of fear, it has no legal right to harm you!

We needn't have a spirit of fear!

1 Corinthians 2:16 says, "'For Who has known the mind of the Lord so as to instruct him?' But we have the mind of Christ" (NIV). He's given us a sound mind through Jesus Christ. He's given us a disciplined mind. He has given us a mind that we might be instructed to do His will. When our minds are focused on Him, His promises, and His love for us, we don't want to focus on fear. Why would we? It's debilitating, and we are made whole through Jesus Christ!

Let the love of God operate in you

When we allow the love of God to operate in our lives, when we walk in His power and authority and when we take on the mind of Jesus Christ, then fear can try to overtake us, but we can overcome!

When we *personally, intimately* know the love of the Father for us, everything changes! **When we know that we are loved unconditionally by the Father who promises to never leave us or forsake us and who is for us and not against us, the spirit of fear is already defeated!**

When you understand the deep, never-ending love of God for you, you will know who you are. You will rest and abide in it. **The love of God for you will be stronger and louder than the spirit of fear can ever be.** God is love and perfect love casts out all fear.

This scripture is SOLID! It sums up living in God's love or the spirit of fear. Let's take a look at it.

> This is how we know that we live in him and he in us: He has given us of his Spirit. And we have seen and testify that the Father has sent his Son to be the Savior of the world. If anyone acknowledges that Jesus is the Son of God, God lives in them and they in God. And so we know and rely on the love God has for us.
>
> God is love. Whoever lives in love lives in God, and God in them. This is how love is made complete among us so that we will have confidence on the day of judgment: In this world we are like Jesus. There is no fear in love. But perfect love drives out fear, because fear has to do with punishment. The one who fears is not made perfect in love. (1 John 4:13–18 NIV)

Abiding in God's love will help you become confident in making decisions. **When you abide in God's love, your decisions will not be manipulated by fear, but your decisions will be based on your trust in your loving God.** Trusting God to lead your every step will move you forward into success in all areas of your life if you follow Him. He will keep you moving into the life He has called you to. But you need to surrender to doing it His way. Surrendering to Him means trusting Him even when you don't understand it or see it His way. His love gives you hope that all things work together for your good because He is in control (Romans 8:28). When you abide in God, fear is gone. Picture yourself living in the tightest, safest, biggest hug of God! Living in that big hug every day is possible, and there is absolutely no room for fear there!

Fear and love cannot co-exist

In the presence of God (perfect love), fear must bow out. **A spirit of fear and love (God) cannot co-exist. You operate from one or the other. You can't live from both spirits**. You can't make decisions based out of both spirits. Your relationships, your work, your family, and your interactions with people cannot succeed and grow if you operate from fear one day and love the next.

God has given you free will to choose. Throughout chapters 28–30 in the book of Deuteronomy, God tells His people to "choose this day" whom they're going to serve. **Today, God still gives you the choice to choose whom you're going to serve—will you choose *fear* or *love*?** Fear brings forth torment, which brings forth death, and love brings peace and life. Choose this day.

As a child of God, you have the relationship and authority in and with Him to rebuke the spirit of fear and to live a life filled with love.

Truth about what He says about you and to you will always trump the lies of the spirit of fear against you. But you have to *believe* His Word and live in it.

I love the lyrics to the song "No Longer Slaves" by Bethel Music. A line from the chorus repeats throughout the song, stating that the speaker is "no longer a slave to fear." What is s/he instead? Simply this: God's child. Being a child of God, and understanding what that means, has the power to cancel out the spirit of fear in a moment!

We do not have to be slaves to fear. Fear has no place. We are God's children. He holds us and our futures in His hands.

Let's work through it…

> ▷ *Are there areas where you may be operating from a spirit of fear rather than from the love of God for you? Name them.*
> ▷ *What do you need to do to kick out that spirit of fear from those areas of your life?*
> ▷ *Does success cause fear or anxiety in you? If so, why and how can you allow God to remove that from you?*
> ▷ *In what ways are you allowing the familiar to pull you back and stop you from becoming all who God called you to be? How can you begin to change that?*

WHAT IS SOMETHING YOU MIGHT BE AFRAID TO SUCCEED IN? TO FAIL IN? HOW DO YOU THINK GOD WANTS YOU TO OVERCOME IN THAT?

25

THE GOAL: KNOW THE FACTS BUT ACTIVATE THE TRUTH

―――――

If you are a believer in Jesus, you know His Word is truth. You know He is truth. In several places in the Word, Jesus states that He is the Way, the Truth and the Life. He tells us we shall know the truth, and the truth will set us free (John 8:32). He tells us He searches for truth in our inward parts. There are countless other scriptures that encourage us to seek and pursue truth. Indeed, there is a lot of emphasis on *truth* in the Word of God.

It's funny, though: I haven't read much about believing in *facts* in the Bible. It doesn't seem to say anywhere that facts will set me free. I haven't heard God tell me to live on facts because they will bring me life. **I haven't seen anything in God's Word which indicates believing the facts would be more beneficial to me than believing the truth found in His Word.**

"But facts are facts!"

Yes, facts are facts. You are correct. But *fact* doesn't make something an absolute *truth*.

Let's look at some examples of what I'm talking about here:

If you lost your job, that's a fact: you lost your job. If you remain in that fact and establish your thoughts based on that fact, you will feel terrible and discouraged, maybe even ashamed and hopeless. If you failed a test, that's a fact. If you lost a game, that's a fact. But what will a focus on facts such as those do for you? Where are God's promises for you in those facts? Does living from *fact* help you or hinder you from living in God's mercies and grace? If you allow yourself to live in facts, fear may set in and down it will all go. If you allow yourself to live in facts, you will never experience the miracles and blessings of God. It's difficult to live in faith while trying to live in facts. **Facts will try to keep you convinced you must be "realistic." Yet truth allows room for God to work out His promises for you.**

But it's a fact. It's a fact I lost my job. How am I supposed to feel or live now? I don't have a job anymore. Where's God in that? What's the truth about that?

Here's how to counteract fact with truth. Hear me now. **It's important that you understand how to navigate through fact vs. truth.** Many live their lives in constant worry and defeat because all they could see are the facts that are overwhelming their lives. But to know there's truth to overcome the fact? That makes life a lot more hopeful.

You lost your job, but the *truth* is you're going to get another one. The truth is there's another job out there for you. That job wasn't the only job on the planet for you. The truth is God already knew it was going to happen. (Remember, He is omniscient—all-knowing.) The truth is, He promises that just as He feeds the birds of the air and clothes the grass and flowers of the fields, He will take care of you (see Matthew 6:25–34). *Truth.* If you trust in God's character and love for you, you know He does not lie, and He fulfills His word. The *fact* is you lost your job, but the *truth* is that God will provide another. So let truth lead you, and do not stay stuck on the fact of the matter.

Find the truth about your situation and lean into that truth

You are His child. You are His very own. He is your good Father. That is all truth. His promises to you are good and can be counted on. He wants to show you that He is truth and He does not lie. What He says He will do.

Let's look at another real-life scenario. The fact might be that you're not getting good grades in school, but the truth is you don't have to continue that way. The truth is you can get yourself a tutor who will help you get the better grade. Or you might have to study more or retake a test. The fact is your grades look bad, but the truth is you have the tools and abilities to turn them around. That is truth vs. fact. The truth is that God will help you and give you the wisdom and understanding you need to overcome that fact if you will allow Him to help you, if you will give of your time and focus to do what is good and honorable to get those grades up. When you honor God, He honors you.

So, can we agree that living from truth is more important and powerful than living from fact? **Just living from facts can hinder you from moving forward, but understanding facts while living from a place of truth will help you move forward.**

How do you live from truth?

In order to live from a place of truth rather than fact, we have to know the Word of God and walk it out. We have to know what He says about our situations. **His Word has *all* the answers in the form of truths.** It is the manual He has provided for us from which to live our lives.

Putting simple principles from God's Word into practice helps us move forward.

> Ask and it will be given to you; seek and you will find; knock and the door will be opened to you. For everyone who asks receives; the one who seeks finds; and to the one who knocks, the door will be opened. (Matthew 7:7–8 NIV)

Put the Word of truth into action!

For example, Matthew 7:7–8 looks like this when it's applied to your life: It's asking God to help you. It's asking the questions. It's asking for another opportunity to change things up. It's about seeking out more help or counsel or study so that you understand things more clearly.

It's seeking truth, accountability and success. It's knocking on the door persistently and doing whatever the Word says to get you where you need to be. *Ask. Seek. Knock.*

This applies to so many areas of life where we need the truth to set us free! **If you follow the ways of truth, you will experience a different life.** Living on facts is hopeless and depressing, in my opinion. Truth gives me hope and freedom!

The fact may be that you're experiencing depression or grief, but the truth is that Jesus came to give you joy and hope. Isaiah 61:3 talks about putting on the garment of praise instead of the spirit of heaviness. If you do what the Word says, you will experience the results of that truth, for the Word of God is truth.

The fact may be that you're in the middle of what seems to be an overwhelming storm, but the truth is that Jesus is able to calm your storm. He has given you peace that the world cannot give, but you must believe Him and allow Him to calm your storm through His peace. Philippians 4:4–9 talks about how we can live in peace. If we apply this truth, the storm will subside. We will make it through!

Operating from a place of truth demands that you *activate* that truth. When you do, the truth will make you free! Knowing God's word is not enough. You cannot merely be a hearer of the Word. If you are, you deceive yourself. You must be a *doer* of the Word so that God can fulfill it.

Be a doer of the Word

Don't just whine about your situation. Don't complain about your life—what's not working, what's not right. Rather, lean into the truth of God's Word and *apply* it. Put the effort in. Do the work. It might be hard at first, but the work will be well worth it in the end. In His truth you will find the answers you're looking for. There is not one situation that God cannot work in and through. **His truth helps you navigate through any facts that can keep you down.** The truth is powerful! Do not discount it or dismiss it.

The following scriptures can inspire and encourage us to live by truth and not by fact.

> If you listen to the Word and don't live out the message you hear, you become like the person who looks in the mirror of the Word to discover the reflection of his face in the beginning. You perceive how God sees you in the mirror of the Word, but then you go out and forget your divine origin. But those who set their gaze deeply into the perfecting law of liberty are fascinated by and respond to the truth they hear and are strengthened by it—they experience God's blessing in all that they do! (James 1:23–25 TPT)

> As the rain and the snow
>   come down from heaven,
> and do not return to it
>   without watering the earth
> and making it bud and flourish,
>   so that it yields seed for the sower and bread for the eater,
> so is my word that goes out from my mouth:
>   It will not return to me empty,
> But will accomplish what I desire
>   and achieve the purpose for which I sent it. (Isaiah 55:10–11 NIV)

> This is why I tell you to never be worried about your life, for all that you need will be provided, such as food, water, clothing—everything your body needs. Isn't there more to your life than a meal? Isn't your body more than clothing?

> Look at all the birds—do you think they worry about their existence? They don't plant or reap or store up food, yet your heavenly Father provides them each with food. Aren't you much more valuable to your Father than they? So, which one of you by worrying could add anything to your life? (Matthew 6:25–27 TPT)

> Know therefore that the LORD your God is God; he is the faithful God, keeping his covenant of love to a thousand generations of those who love him and keep his commandments. (Deuteronomy 7:9 NIV)

This question will help you get started on becoming free to live in the truth: "What is truth? Right here, right now. In the middle of *this*, what is truth?"

What you decide will rule. Will it be fact or truth?

Let's work through it...

Living from facts can leave you accepting certain things God never intended for you to live in. Get with God and allow Him to speak into your life and show you the truth of the matter. He is faithful. He is real. He wants to lead your life through His truth and set you free!

> ▷ *What "facts" in your life currently feel negative or discouraging?*
> ▷ *What is the truth that counteracts the fact you may be dealing with today?*
> ▷ *What does trusting Him in the face of those facts look like?*

HOW MUCH FREER AND LIGHTER WOULD YOU BE IF YOU CHOSE TO LIVE FROM TRUTH, EVEN IF IT'S MORE EFFORT TO DO SO?

Important Baby Steps to Fulfill Your Dreams

Goals:

- ▶ Know and operate from your personal core values
- ▶ Write it down

ACTIVATE YOUR VISION WITH A MISSION AND GOALS

26

THE GOAL: KNOW AND OPERATE FROM YOUR PERSONAL CORE VALUES

What are your likes? Your dislikes? Your strengths? Your weaknesses? What makes you upset? Sad? What makes you laugh? What gives you fulfillment? What are your natural giftings? What are your convictions, morally? Spiritually? What are your thoughts or opinions on issues that matter that might make a difference? Who are your friends? Who are your main influences? Why do you make the decisions you do? What's important to you at the end of the day?

So many questions... **But these kinds of questions help you begin the process of discovering *at the core*, who you really are, on the inside.**

As we've looked at in previous sessions, it doesn't start by what you do, but rather who God made you to be. So, let's get to the heart of this by beginning with your personal core values.

What is a personal core value?

Personal core values are the general expression of what is most important to you. A *value* expresses the worth of something, and in this case, what you categorically like and dislike. So, personal core values are like categories for all your preferences in life.

I appreciate these quotes and insights from Scott Jeffrey on the importance of core values in his article, "7 Steps to Discovering Your Personal Core Values."

> *Values are a part of us. They highlight what we stand for. They can represent our unique, individual essence. Values guide our behavior, providing us with a personal code of conduct. When we honor our personal core values consistently, we experience fulfillment.*
>
> *Values aren't selected; they're discovered. We don't choose our values. Our values reveal themselves to us.*[4]

Take some time and think about this: **at the end of the day, would you honestly be able to say that you respected and lived by your own core values?** All your choices, decisions, thoughts and words: do they come from your personal core value system?

Taking the time to explore the questions listed at the beginning of this session and being really honest about how you're living and what you're doing with your personal core values will reveal what makes you, you.

What is a core value?

Core values are those things that are important to you on a daily basis. **Every decision or choice we make is based on our core values, whether we're aware of them or not.**

Let's look at some everyday, common examples.

One of my core values is INTEGRITY. If I'm offered a job that requires me to steal, I won't take the job. Why? Because stealing goes against my core value of having integrity. If I have integrity, no matter how much that job pays, what status it will give me, or what the benefits are, I will not take it if it requires me to steal. It will go against the integrity that

---

[4] Scott Jeffrey, "7 Steps to Discovering Your Personal Core Values," CEOSage, June 25, 2020, https://scottjeffrey.com/personal-core-values/.

makes up the kind of person I am. So, my core value of integrity in action becomes about *who* I am and not what I *do*.

On the other hand, if my core value is integrity and I do take the job that is asking me to steal, what will happen to me? How will I feel, day after day? How will I operate? What will happen to me? I will feel awful. I will always be on edge, unhappy, frustrated, afraid, angry, depressed etc… Why? Because I would be allowing my core value of integrity to be compromised. When our core values are compromised, we don't live out the authentic person we are and so we live 'off', not right, not true to ourselves. And then life becomes confusing and unfulfilling.

Another example: If being ORGANIZED is a core value of mine, and I can never find my papers because the roommates I live with are messy and are disrespectful of my space, the mismatch between their actions and my core value of living in a well-organized space will affect me, and I won't be able to function successfully. My core value of being organized will have been compromised, and I will need to get things back into order or I'll be the one to be a mess!

We live from our core values. Our core values manifest how God designed us. Our core values reveal our personalities and how we live our lives. We are different from each other; we are each unique.

Based on your core values, you will see the person you are uncovering, the real you, who you truly are. Everyone is different. We can't compare ourselves to others. We are each called to live our purposes out in unique ways. We are to stay true to our authentic selves.

Look at what you like, what you don't like, what you will tolerate and accept and what you will not. Determine what kind of relationships you're attracted to and what kind of jobs will keep you, how you react or respond to people and situations. You can use those core values to start making clearer, more precise decisions in all areas of your life. Once you know and become more aware of living from your core values, you will better understand the *why* behind the decisions and choices you've made and are making. The why now becomes so important and it becomes a strong stepping stone to continue growing a stronger and more meaningful life.

James Clear, *New York Times* bestselling author of *Atomic Habits*, offers a list of core values "commonly used by leadership institutes and programs. This list is not exhaustive, but it will give you an idea of some common core values (also called personal values)." When choosing your core values, focus on what truly is important to you. Keep the list realistic and fairly short. I personally suggest listing off seven top core values. Then, you can go from there after you've given yourself enough time to be really aware of those top seven in your daily living. As Clear points out to his readers, **"if everything is a core value, then nothing is really a priority."**[5] Here is Clear's list:

Core Values List

- Authenticity
- Achievement
- Adventure
- Authority
- Autonomy
- Balance
- Beauty
- Boldness
- Compassion
- Challenge
- Citizenship
- Community
- Competency
- Contribution
- Creativity
- Curiosity
- Determination
- Fairness

---

[5] James Clear, "Core Values List: Over 50 Common Personal Values," James Clear, June 12, 2018, https://jamesclear.com/core-values.

- Faith
- Fame
- Friendships
- Fun
- Growth
- Happiness
- Honesty
- Humor
- Influence
- Inner Harmony
- Justice
- Kindness
- Knowledge
- Leadership
- Learning
- Love
- Loyalty
- Meaningful Work
- Openness
- Optimism
- Peace
- Pleasure
- Poise
- Popularity
- Recognition
- Religion
- Reputation
- Respect
- Responsibility
- Security
- Self-Respect
- Service
- Spirituality
- Stability
- Success
- Status

- Trustworthiness
- Wealth
- Wisdom

Let's work through it...

List seven of your core values:

1.
2.
3.
4.
5.
6.
7.

After you've listed your seven top core values, look at each one. Assess how each works its way into your life, into your thought patterns, your choices, your decisions, and your way of living.

Take a moment and look over your core values and ponder the following questions.

> ▷ *How do these core values affect your home life? Your job or/and schooling? Your relationships? Your spiritual life? Your habits?*

In regard to making a decision about, for example, a career or a relationship, you might want to measure that decision against your core values to see if it fits who you are.

Your core values reveal the type of person you are, what tasks you're willing to accomplish, what relationship you're going to get into, what kind of environment you'd like to work in, what job description you're equipped to fulfill, and so on.

Be aware of *why* you make the choices you make, how you make them, why you pursue the relationships you pursue, and so on. Be aware of your *self* and what makes you, you. This awareness will give you courage to help you be the authentic you God created you to be.

Listing your core values and honestly reflecting on how they are being respected or compromised can help you change your life or help you navigate differently through it.

AT THE END OF THE DAY, YOU WANT TO BE ABLE TO LAY YOUR HEAD ON THE PILLOW AND KNOW THAT YOU'VE STAYED TRUE TO YOUR CONVICTIONS, MORALS AND PASSIONS.

27

THE GOAL: WRITE IT DOWN!

———

This session is a bit more hands-on. To fully understand what a vision is, you'll need to physically begin putting this session into action in your daily life.

Your vision of your future should get you excited. **Your vision should cause you to get up in the morning and say, "I *get* to do this today. I don't *have* to, but I *get* to!"** When you come home after a day of working within that vision, you say, "I got to do this today, and tomorrow I get to do it all over again!" That brings joy to your heart.

Let's work through it…

If you're not sure what your vision is, start with questions such as these to begin to define one:

- What do you want to do with your life?
- What makes you feel alive?
- Who do you want to reach?
- Who do you want to impact?
- What goals do you want to accomplish through it?
- What legacy will you leave behind?

Your vision should also be able to answer all the typical journalist questions about it. Here they are:

Who is involved in the vision?
What is the vision's purpose?
Why does the vision exist?
Where does the vision take place?
When does the vision take place? (is this a one-time thing? For years to come…?)
How will the vision operate to sustain itself?

A vision cannot just stay a vision when it's something you know you're called to and you feel it in your bones. A true vision is one you dream about becoming reality, and then when you put wings to it, it flies. **The vision becomes reality when you determine to work hard and put feet, hands or a mouth to it**. A vision speaks, and it goes, and it works to produce what you desire it to be and do.

God had a vision

Have you ever thought about God having a vision or being a visionary? (I wonder what His vision board looked like just before He created the earth?) The Bible talks about God having a dream that no one perish, but all come to repentance and have eternal life (2 Peter 3:9). That was one of God's greatest visions for mankind. His vision included a perfect, loving, intimate relationship with each of us for all of eternity. But then that thing—sin—happened. Did His vision die then? No, not at all! God fought for His original vision to be fulfilled, and He worked it out so that it happened!

If I may put it this way, it is like God put work and effort into his vision. Through the plan He created of salvation through Jesus Christ, His vision became reality.

His vision was launched through His core values of love, kindness, patience, forgiveness, creativity, organization, originality…God has a GREAT value system!

What should my vision look like?

God created us to have vision, to have a calling to fulfill just like He did and does. I can't overstress this point: He created us in His image, and we reflect Him and all He's about—even through our visions!

Our visions should look like His vision since we're created in his image. So, that means your vision should include some of the following considerations:

- Your vision should be God-centered and purpose-full.
- Your vision should be effective and productive.
- Your vision should fuel you with joy not dread as you work it through.
- Your vision should be created from your passion and skills.
- Your vision should launch from your core values and be sustained by your efforts and hard work.
- Your vision should be something that when people see it, they see you all over it—who you are, how you think, what you love. It should have your personal signature all over it.
- Your vision should have the fingerprints of God over it, that people would see God's love and purposes all over it.

Consider writing down your vision. Then, map how your core values match that vision.

Some more questions to consider while mapping out your vision: How can your vision bring glory to God? What are your motives behind it? Let Holy Spirit walk it through with you and see how He wants to work it *with* you.

Let's take a look at Habakkuk 2:2–3.

> Then the LORD answered me and said:
> "Write the vision
> And make it plain on tablets,
> That he may run who reads it.
> For the vision is yet for an appointed time;

But at the end it will speak, and it will not lie.
Though it tarries, wait for it;
Because it will surely come,
It will not tarry." (NKJV)

Write down your vision and run with it. Don't give up. Work hard and diligently on it. Do what needs to be done without complaining. Don't be discouraged if it doesn't happen overnight. Don't rush it. God's timing is always the right timing. Surrender your vision to God and let Him help you work it. Let Holy Spirit breathe life into it!

Write it in detail. Pray over it. Ask God to lead you to accomplish it with His guidance and His wisdom. Be open to having God tweak it over the days and weeks to come until you feel His peace over it.

Creating or writing your vision out based on an understanding of your core values will help you sustain your vision long-term. It won't just be something you want to do because it's a great idea or someone encouraged you to do it. It will be a vision birthed from the inside of you, and only you can make it and keep it uniquely yours for as long as you want to. You can't produce authentic, lasting results if you don't know the core values God placed within you (making you the original, unique person you are). You function out of your core values every day, and through pursuing your vision, you tell the world: *This is who I am. This is what's important to me! This is what I am called to do!*

Let's work through it...

   ▷ *Do you have a vision? (Note: we can have multiple visions which affect multiple areas of our lives.) For example, do you have a vision for your career? A vision for your marriage? A vision for your budget goals?*
   ▷ *Is your vision realistic: has it been created from your own skills, giftings and passion?*
   ▷ *Write one vision down at a time including some or all of the questions and considerations we just went through. As you begin*

to write it out, sit with Holy Spirit and have ears to hear what He is saying to you about it.

▷ *When you write your vision, ask yourself the Journalist questions listed in this session as well. They will help you write it out in greater clarity.*

WHAT IS ONE THING YOU CAN DO NOW TO BEGIN MOVING TOWARDS MAKING YOUR VISION A REALITY?

28

THE GOAL: ACTIVATE YOUR VISION WITH A MISSION AND GOALS

———

This session, like the last, needs your hands-on participation in order for your vision to happen.

People think when they have a vision, it's just going to happen. If you're one of those people, I'm sorry if I'm bursting your bubble, but it's not just going to happen.

You may have an awesome, world-changing vision that has the potential to bring you to places you can't even imagine right now, but if you don't have the perseverance to carry out the vision, and if you're not using the right tools to establish the vision and make it excellent and useful, it will never happen.

In order to see a vision become more than a dream, you must be on mission. **Mission activates vision.**

An example may make this concept clearer:

Let's say my vision is to build 100 schools in a certain part of Africa so that all children living near those schools have the opportunity for an education which will give them a better life. You may applaud me and tell me what a great vision I have. You may ask God to bless me for being a compassionate person, willing to help children. Thank you. Great. But so what? **Me sharing my vision with you and the applause you give me for what I *want* to accomplish is not going to actually get it done. I need more than a dream and cheerleaders. I need to be on a mission to activate my vision to see it become reality.**

What does a mission look like?

A *mission* is a general picture that includes all of what is needed to make the vision a reality. So let me paint the picture of my mission for what my vision needs to include. It would look like this (these points are not meant to be all-inclusive, but some things I need to start establishing that will begin to activate my vision):

- A board of directors or a committee to help me facilitate all aspects of this project
- A fundraising campaign to raise money for the different needs of this vision
- A real estate agent in the area to purchase land on which to build the schools
- Engineers, builders, etc., to build the schools
- Permits, etc., so that I can operate a legal school program
- A lawyer to work on all the legal aspects of it
- Work visas to be able to send teachers out to the field
- Gather Teachers willing to work there
- Establish the curriculum that will serve the students well within their culture
- Make lists to purchase school supplies, clothing, etc., so students have all they need to succeed

Et cetera, et cetera, et cetera.

Now that I have an overall, general picture of the mission I created, I now need goals to accomplish and establish that mission. A mission needs goals, and goals need a mission! Big goals. Small goals. **Goals fuel the mission to activate the vision.**

To accomplish a mission, defined goals must be set

A mission can be broken down into GOALS—big goals and smaller goals. To each goal, I usually attach a deadline. The deadline holds me accountable to accomplish the goal in a timely and realistic manner. Often, I can't accomplish the next goal until I fulfill the one right before it. Setting goals and timelines for my mission reminds me that I can't skip some if I'm going to work towards making the vision one that is both sustainable and excellent.

A mission with goals feeds life to the vision. A mission sets me on course to intelligently, realistically and spiritually look into and provide all that is needed to fulfill the vision.

Goals should not overwhelm you. They should bring you a sense of peace and empowerment. They enable you to fulfill each step of the mission, one step at a time, to see the vision come to pass.

Let's work through it...

> ▷ *Write down your mission that will turn your vision into a reality*
> ▷ *Write down the bigger and smaller goals that will accomplish your mission*
> ▷ *Are you willing to set goals and respect them?*

WHAT OR WHO ARE YOU ACCOUNTABLE TO, TO ENSURE YOU MEET YOUR MISSION GOALS?

WRAP-UP SESSION (BUT KEEP GOING!)

THE GOAL: LET HIM LEAD YOU

There's something about being cared for by the powerful, almighty, yet kind and gentle God that leaves me feeling at peace and comforted.

> The LORD is my shepherd;
>> I have all that I need.
> He lets me rest in green meadows;
>> he leads me beside peaceful streams.
>> He renews my strength.
> He guides me along right paths,
>> bringing honor to his name.
> Even when I walk
>> through the darkest valley,
> I will not be afraid,
>> for you are close beside me.
> Your rod and your staff
>> protect and comfort me.
> You prepare a feast for me
>> in the presence of my enemies.
> You honor me by anointing my head with oil.
>> My cup overflows with blessings.
> Surely your goodness and unfailing love will pursue me
>> all the days of my life,
> and I will live in the house of the LORD
>> forever. (Psalm 23 NLT)

The Bible compares us to sheep at times. I'm not sure I like that description or comparison! I'd rather be compared to a lion or a dove, something powerful or beautiful! But a sheep? Not my preference. But I see why we are...

Consider the following facts about sheep. You may be surprised to find yourself in one of them, in any or all of these scenarios! But you will also find how loving and caring Jesus is as your perfect Shepherd.

Get out of the rut

A sheep will walk around and around and around the same path until it creates a rut. A *rut* by definition is "a long deep track made by the repeated passage of the wheels of vehicles; a habit or pattern of behavior that has become dull and unproductive but is hard to change."[6]

When a sheep falls into a rut, it normally cannot get out by itself. It's in too deep. The sheep needs the Shepherd to come get it out. Isn't that interesting? Doesn't it sound the same as most of us who get into ruts? We need Jesus to come get us out!

Our rut sometimes consists of our flesh warring against the spirit. We may find ourselves continually doing the things we don't want to do.

> For I do not do the good I want to do, but the evil I do not want to do— this I keep on doing. Now if I do what I do not want to do, it is no longer I who do it, but it is sin living in me that does it. (Romans 7:19–20 NIV)

That's why it's important to grow in Christ and to "walk in the Holy Spirit" so we don't keep doing things that will keep us stuck (in our sin) or hold us back from all God has for us.

Let me be clear, Jesus has set us free—not partially, but completely and wonderfully free! We must always cherish this truth and stubbornly refuse to go back into the bondage of our past.

---

[6] "Rut." Lexico Dictionaries – English, Accessed March 25, 2020, https://www.lexico.com/en/definition/rut.

As you yield freely and fully to the dynamic life and power of the Holy Spirit, you will abandon the cravings of your self-life. For your self-life craves the things that offend the Holy Spirit and hinder him from living free within you! And the Holy Spirit's intense cravings hinder your old self-life from dominating you! So then, the two incompatible and conflicting forces within you are your self-life of the flesh and the new creation life of the Spirit. But when you are brought into the full freedom of the Spirit of grace, you will no longer be living under the domination of the law, but soaring above it! (Galatians 5:16–18 TPT)

Our flesh wants to keep us in a rut, but the Holy Spirit calls us to a different way of living in freedom!

I've fallen and can't get back up!

When sheep fall on their backs, they normally can't get back up by themselves. They need a shepherd to come put them back right side up on their four legs. If they lay on their backs for a long period of time and don't get help, they will eventually die. Laying in that position for too long begins to affect the function of their organs. Isn't that interesting? When we fall, sometimes it's hard to get back up, or it's tempting just to stay there. We fear, we're ashamed, we feel guilty… Why did we fall in the first place, right? Condemnation and weakness cause us to keep laying there, and we feel unable to or don't even want to get back up. Staying down too long could lead to hopelessness, depression and defeat, which becomes a great invitation for the enemy to come in and leave us for dead. So, when we're down, we need to call for the Shepherd Jesus to come put us back right side up! There's too much life for us to live for. We must allow Jesus to help us stand up and walk again!

The LORD upholds all who fall and lifts up all who are bowed down. (Psalm 145:14 NIV)

Get out of my head!

Flies and other insects, if not controlled, are likely to get into a sheep's head. Literally—they get into the sheep's head through its eye ducts, nose or ears. The intrusion of the bugs can cause such pain that the sheep will find a rock to beat its head on to try to release the pain. Again, when we allow the "flies"—the lies of the enemy—to intrude into our minds, if those lies are not dealt with, they can drive us to tormenting pain and even death! Death of hope, dreams and life. That's the enemy's ultimate goal—to kill us. Be aware of his schemes!

So what does the Shepherd do for the sheep so that the flies and bugs don't invade? He makes an ointment with oil and other ingredients. He then rubs the ointment into the sheep's head, around its eyes, nose and ears to keep the pestering bugs away.

So it is with Jesus, our Shepherd, and us: He anoints our heads with oil, which is His Holy Spirit, and He covers our minds with Him, His Word, His truth so that the pestering bugs of the enemy cannot penetrate and intrude our minds with lies.

Stop imitating the ideals and opinions of the culture around you, but be inwardly transformed by the Holy Spirit through a total reformation of how you think.

> Therefore, I urge you, brothers and sisters, in view of God's mercy, to offer your bodies as a living sacrifice, holy and pleasing to God—this is your true and proper worship. Do not conform to the pattern of this world, but be transformed by the renewing of your mind. This will empower you to discern God's will as you live a beautiful life, satisfying and perfect in his eyes. (Romans 12:1–2 TPT)

We cannot get lazy and allow "whatever" (negative or evil) to pass through and even stay in our souls (mind, emotions and will). We need to be proactive and keep our souls clean before God so that the lies (flies) of the enemy don't have a place to land and cause torment. Remember, we can't keep the doors open to the enemy. It's just not worth it, and it's not how God intended for us to live. When those lies come to flood our minds, we need to activate 2 Corinthians 10:5—"We demolish arguments and every pretension that sets itself up against the knowledge of God, and we take captive every thought to make it obedient to Christ" (NIV).

Hungry for Him

His desire is to lead us to green pastures so that we can eat of His rich, nourishing Word, which will sustain us through whatever life throws at us. He alone can satisfy us. He alone can satisfy our hunger for truth and for abundant life.

Just like I encouraged you to be careful what your soul takes in, I want to encourage you to be aware of what you're "eating" as well. What "food" are you eating that is filling you up and nurturing you? What is making you stronger as a believer in Jesus? We all know that too much sugar, the wrong carbs, caffeine, and those kinds of foods are not the greatest to fuel and sustain our bodies, but we keep eating them. Before long, we start to experience all sorts of pains and trouble, and eventually, we have to change our diets. The same goes for our spiritual inner man as we grow in Christ. We can't grow healthy and strong if we're not eating of the Word of God daily. And we can't go on last Sunday's sermon, either, or a once-a-week YouTube surf for a "good message."

Remember the story of God's people, the Israelites, as they crossed the desert from Egypt? God sent them manna from heaven to feed them. Manna from heaven itself! It must have been exciting to see it fall from the skies. But after a while, the people got lazy. They started grumbling because they had to go gather it fresh every single day if they wanted to eat. They weren't allowed to get it all at once for the week. They had to go out and get the fresh stuff every single day. If they banked on eating what they'd gathered the day before, they would find it molded and gross! I think God was trying to give us the message that He wants us to get our spiritual food fresh from Him every single day. It's called relationship. He's not a once-a-week grocery delivery man. He is God our Father, and He wants to nourish us with His love and mercies that are new every morning.

> But Jesus told him, "No! The Scriptures say, 'People do not live by bread alone, but by every word that comes from the mouth of God.'" (Matthew 4:4 NLT)

Then Jesus declared, "I am the bread of life. Whoever comes to me will never go hungry, and whoever believes in me will never be thirsty." (John 6:35 NIV)

Lead me, please

He desires to lead us to still waters and to His peace. Only as we allow Him to lead us, and we follow will we end up in the place He desires for us to be. Only as we allow Him to lead us will we find ourselves in a place of safety in the middle of the storms of life. We need to trust Him to lead us even if the path seems unfamiliar. We need to learn to hold on tightly to His hand and be led through the dark. He is our light. He is our peace. He orders our every step. We can trust Him.

The LORD directs the steps of the godly. He delights in every detail of their lives. (Psalm 37:23 NLT)

In a world where we experience so many different emotions, it's tempting to allow our feelings to lead us. But feelings aren't stable. They change from moment to moment. It's a scary thing to be led by emotions! I encourage you to be led by the peace of God. How can you get that peace when so much chaos is filling our minds and our world? Let's take a look at Philippians 4: 6–9 (NLT):

Don't worry about anything; instead, pray about everything. Tell God what you need, and thank him for all he has done. Then you will experience God's peace, which exceeds anything we can understand. His peace will guard your hearts and minds as you live in Christ Jesus. And now, dear brothers and sisters, one final thing. Fix your thoughts on what is true, and honorable, and right, and pure, and lovely, and admirable. Think about things that are excellent and worthy of praise. Keep putting into practice all you learned and received from me—everything you heard from me and saw me doing. Then the God of peace will be with you.

When you put your trust in God (I know that's not always easy to do), you will experience His perfect peace. When peace overtakes you, you can be led by Him because you will not be spiraling out of control, and you will not be fearful or anxious. You will hear His voice lead you in the right direction, on the right path. He reminds us in John 10 that His sheep (there's that comparison again!) know His voice. If we know His voice, we can follow it in confidence.

He's a good Shepherd and will never lead you off a cliff!

Restoration

He restores our soul. He is able to bring healing and hope where there was pain and despair. And even in the middle of strife and brokenness with people around us and with our enemies, He is able to protect us and comfort us.

Sometimes it feels as though restoration or healing is impossible. But is it? When you think about who Jesus is and what He went through, is it really impossible? All that Jesus went through—the mocking, betrayal, beatings unto death on the cross—through it all, He was able to forgive and love. Wow… And He has given His Spirit and His strength to help us. And when we rely on Him and walk with Him, restoration and healing come no matter what or how we've been wounded, rejected or misunderstood. If there's anyone who understands, it's Jesus. He's been there. Because He has, His compassion towards you abounds. Let His healing in. Let His promises for hope and healing saturate you as you learn to trust Him. Be patient with yourself. Sometimes it takes longer than you want it to, but healing and restoration will come.

> Those who hope in the LORD will renew their strength. They will soar on wings like eagles; they will run and not grow weary, they will walk and not be faint. (Isaiah 40:31 NIV)

> And the God of all grace, who called you to his eternal glory in Christ, after you have suffered a little while, will himself restore you and make you strong, firm and steadfast. (1 Peter 5:10 NIV)

Like sheep, we need Jesus!

Do you see why God calls us *sheep* in the Bible? We are so much like sheep. We need so much help from our loving, patient Shepherd.

We get into ruts, we fall down, we allow the enemy to lie to us, and we just get ourselves in over our heads sometimes to our own hurt. Oh, how we need Jesus to help us!

We could hire many counselors and life coaches to advise us and to direct us. We can read many self-help books to help us live a successful and comfortable life. We can do our very best to achieve our own goals and win. This is all good and noble, but without Jesus, none of these things will sustain us. Jesus is our life-giver. Without Him, we are empty! We need Him! He is our constant and will never fail us.

Let's work through it...

> ▷ *How are you being led by Jesus? Where is He taking you?*
> ▷ *How can you trust Jesus as your Shepherd?*
> ▷ *Are you allowing Him to anoint your head with His oil?*
> ▷ *How are you allowing Him to restore your soul? What does that look like?*
> ▷ *What are you feeding off of? What waters are you drinking from?*

I encourage you to look deeper into the shepherd/sheep relationship in the book *A Shepherd Looks at Psalm 23* by Phillip Keller.

No matter where you are on your journey with Jesus, know that He will never leave you. He will always be everything you need. You can count on Him. Remember, you are His very own precious one.

CONCLUSION

Can I remind you how much God loves you? Yeah. He really does. Don't ever doubt that. There is nothing or anyone that can ever take God's love from you.

> If God is for us, who can ever be against us? Since he did not spare even his own Son but gave him up for us all, won't he also give us everything else? Who dares accuse us whom God has chosen for his own? No one—for God himself has given us right standing with himself. Who then will condemn us? No one—for Christ Jesus died for us and was raised to life for us, and he is sitting in the place of honor at God's right hand, pleading for us.
>
> Can anything ever separate us from Christ's love? Does it mean he no longer loves us if we have trouble or calamity, or are persecuted, or hungry, or destitute, or in danger, or threatened with death? (As the Scriptures say, "For your sake we are killed every day; we are being slaughtered like sheep.") No, despite all these things, overwhelming victory is ours through Christ, who loved us.
>
> And I am convinced that nothing can ever separate us from God's love. Neither death nor life, neither angels nor demons, neither our fears for today nor our worries about tomorrow—not even the powers of hell can separate us from God's love. No power in the sky above or in the earth below—indeed, nothing in all creation will ever be able to separate us from the love of God that is revealed in Christ Jesus our Lord. (Romans 8:31–39 NLT)

I pray that all you have read has encouraged you to keep going. Keep moving forward, don't quit. Run the race well. God is forever faithful. Rest and trust in His goodness. He is your good Shepherd. His thoughts *abound* towards you!

Based on all the truths you have found in this book, be empowered to not only exist, but to truly LIVE!

For booking information for Life Coaching, Workshops
and Speaking opportunities please visit livingitreal.life

CPSIA information can be obtained
at www.ICGtesting.com
Printed in the USA
BVHW071020210921
617187BV00002B/106